MY DOG IS
My Relationship Coach

MAUREEN SCANLON

outskirts
press

Outskirts Press, Inc.
http://www.outskirtspress.com

ISBN: 978-1-9772-3686-9

Library of Congress Control Number: 2020924496

Cover Photo © 2021 Johni Cesario @ HTTPS://UNCOVERINGFLORA.COM.
All rights reserved - used with permission.

Outskirts Press and the "OP" logo are trademarks belonging to Outskirts Press, Inc.

PRINTED IN THE UNITED STATES OF AMERICA

NOTE FROM THE AUTHOR

Today is the day I decided it was time. My furry babies, Jade (the chihuahua), Brodie (the Aussie), along with a new addition, Callie, my daughter's border collie, are lying on the couch taking naps and they have no idea they are once more going to be the stars of a self-help book. They are just happy we are all in the same room and they sleep peacefully (even snoring) as I excitedly head into the next step of our journey together.

I reflect back to five years ago. Sitting in my bed, I had just ended another relationship. I dated this particular person for a year, even with a proposal on a Hawaiian beach, but alas, it didn't last. I cried, felt anger, confusion, and frustration at the "why" of another failed attempt at lifelong love. The furry babies, Brodie and Jade, lie on the bed, come to me, and lick my face and get as close as possible. This is their way of comforting my sorrow and letting me know THEY love me. I don't need to be perfect because in their eyes I already am. THIS is why dogs are more enlightened and they ARE **relationship experts**. It is simple, pure, unconditional love. They remind me of my worth as I embark on the pursuit of happiness and a true love that will last.

I am so excited to begin this new journey into the second book in what is now a series of "**My Dog Is...**" books. After writing my first book, *My Dog Is More Enlightened Than I Am*, I was asked a lot of questions in relation to marriage, dating, and relationships. In keeping with the premise of how enlightened our furry pets are, I realized, once again, they have a lot to teach about a variety of subjects.

We will explore how they can enhance our view of relationships and the easy methods we can use to find and keep the meaningful relationships we are seeking.

On our search for love, companionship, and "the one," we oftentimes lose sight and alignment with our true selves and what we deeply desire in a life partner. This book will help you to see clearly what it takes to heal yourself, enhance your marriage and romantic relationships, and realize the whole person you were meant to be while in a relationship, in marriage, or searching for that perfect mate.

This book will be more forthright, with my own sometimes painful, but raw and honest journey to finding love. With tips, examples, and anecdotes, along with my own experiences, I will share with you the meaning, clarity, and deep connections we can all take to enhance the journey of finding or loving "our person."

I appreciate each and every reader! My hope and message are always that you will have, be, and do all that you came into this world to accomplish and live your most fulfilled life!

ACKNOWLEDGMENTS
AND DEDICATION

First and foremost, I must dedicate this book to my most loving, supportive, encouraging, and perfect-for-me husband, Dennis.

Since this is a book about romance, love, marriage, and finding our match, it is only fitting that I would dedicate this to him.

Dennis—Your belief and uplifting love have been nothing short of miraculous. They say you'll just know when you meet the one for you. I knew when I met you that you felt like home. I had no idea the growth and journey we would take together and how our energies and connection would flow. I now know the meaning of a Twin Flame, two souls walking the earth or lifetime separately until the time is meant to join once again. I love me with you!

To my amazing children, Lacee, Jordania, and Noah—As I lived my life I strived to show you unconditional love. I wanted you to carry this into the world and understand the worth and beauty you each have. I am so proud of each of you! I see strength, kindness, courage, love, and self-confidence in you all. I know that you three will contribute to the world in such a beautiful way. Thank you for choosing me to be your mother! I wish for true, unconditionally loving partners for each of you!

To Noemi and Kris—Thank you for being my son and my daughter's persons. I am so very happy with the choices they have made to love you and add you to our family. I am so happy to have a bonus daughter and a bonus son. Love you both!

To my precious grandbabies, Aiden, Paisley, and Braylynn—I hope one day you all find a love that you deserve. I hope that we guide you to know your worth and the beautiful souls of greatness you are! I write these for you in hopes of leaving a legacy of love, kindness, and compassion that you will one day remember your Grandma Maureen taught you. Hugs and kisses, my loves.

To my amazing friends—

Linda, we are soul sisters (tattoos to prove it) and this journey has been so fun with you in it. We have leaned on, cried, laughed, and loved each other during so many phases of this life and we have so much more to go. We are soul family.

Laura—From teenage friends to adult moms, our connection never changed. You were and are so amazing. I love your humor and how genuinely you love those in your life. Your support has been appreciated more than words can say. Friends Forever

To the many others who influence and teach me every day, to my Life Coaching clients, friends who have been by my side and never fail to show up – my circle is small but mighty!

TABLE OF CONTENTS

Chapter 1

WHY ARE WE TOGETHER?

As I begin this book, I want to state this—life can be messy, disorganized, unexpected, disappointing, and downright confusing. This is what makes it fun and challenging. You wouldn't want to put together a puzzle you had already completed 100 times before, or answer a riddle that you already knew the punch line to, so let's look at the journey of finding, growing, and keeping a romantic relationship in the same way. Enjoy the ride!

Because there are so many varieties of relationships, the chapters in this book will address a plethora of these in a random and spontaneous order. I believe we can all learn from and help one another in each stage of life, so on with this new adventure...

If you are currently in a marriage or relationship, or considering reuniting with an ex-partner, or in the beginning stage of dating someone new, I think this is the most important question to ask yourself:

"Do I truly love this person or the idea of the person I want them to be?"

Let's break that down into several mini questions and statements:

a) Does it seem like a struggle or "work" every single time we are together?

b) We have been together so long; I don't want to give up.

c) The more effort I give to this, the bigger the reward if he/she can change.

d) Am I lost in the fantasy of #relationship goals (the millennial version of "that's the relationship I wish I had")?

e) Do I have to seek things I like about them?

f) Do I love this person at their worst or only at their best?

g) It's an "us against the world" view.

h) The excuse list (a bad quality that is then followed by a "but"): ...*but* he is a good dad; ...*but* she works hard; he's difficult *but*...; yeah, but, but... (I call this being the Yabbut Rabbit)

i) And the biggie... Are we together just because I do not want to be alone?

I would be doing a disfavor to my readers to speak of relationships without mentioning the very common and dysfunctional relationship traits that everyone should be aware of and avoid. I will just dive right in.

First, and of foremost importance, NEVER ACCEPT ABUSE, period. Whether it's physical, emotional, or psychological, remove yourself and detach. Find a support system, community help, hotline, charity organization, or medical professional; please speak up and get help!

Abuse is **never** a part of a healthy relationship. That means not sometimes, occasionally, or when they drink, are stressed, etc. **Never** means **Never Ever!**

If you are not sure you are experiencing abuse, ask someone. Share with friends and family to get an objective view. There are different kinds of abuse, not just physical. Do NOT feel ashamed if you are unclear. Listen to your feelings and be wary of the words you are being told.

If you have been isolated from friends and family, call them.

Abuse is never okay. There is NO correlation between love and abuse except manipulation and control.

I am a formerly abused spouse, and I have a daughter who escaped an abusive marriage as well; therefore, I really understand the crippling emotional, financial, and physical fear associated with it. Yes, hindsight is 20/20, so I must share these words and urge anyone in an unhealthy relationship to seek out and tell someone and get help.

I once saw a video where an abused woman convinced her abuser that she needed to take her dog to a veterinarian in an attempt to leave her abuser. Unfortunately, her abuser went with her and had a gun in his pocket. She heroically slipped a note to the receptionist while at the visit, pleading to have her call 911. She found a way! What courage and strength it took to do that for herself!

That is one of the beautiful stories of a thriver (not just a survivor) of abuse.

I turn to addressing married couples and how to tell if your marriage needs work or if it is time to part ways for your emotional health.

In a marriage, there are four key factors to consider:

Trust

Honesty

Intimacy

Financial

You do not see love in this list. Love is (or was) present for you when you decided to become partners. I now say, love is secondary if the other factors are not there. However, if there is no love present, we do not need to go further with the other four factors.

a) **Do I trust my spouse with everything? Yes, everything.** Could your spouse look through your social media, your phone, your car, or even your mail without you feeling anxiety? If so, you have a very high level of trust. If not, you have some work to do. This is a good measurement of the need to dig deep and see what it is you are hiding and why.

   If there is a fear of sharing with your spouse, is it because you are afraid of their reaction or are you doing something you know is not honoring your partnership with him/her? Can you trust them with your unlocked phone when you leave the room? Do they have your passwords? Could they open your mail? I am not saying this is necessary, as many of us view it as a breach of our privacy, but COULD you?

b) **Oh, honestly.** How much do you share about your daily life? Your health? Your most intimate dreams, hopes, fears? Do you tell your spouse everything, leaving no stone unturned? Do you feel safe sharing your deepest thoughts and feelings?

My husband and I watched a wonderful series on NETFLIX called *Living With Yourself* starring Paul Rudd. The synopsis of the series is that the main character, Miles, goes to a spa that is recommended by a coworker. He spends $50,000 to get a DNA scrub, wakes up in a grave after an attempt to bury him alive, and realizes he was cloned. He meets his clone, who is a better version of himself. He grows to dislike the clone because the clone really loves the life Miles has taken for granted.

As we were watching, we looked over at one another and asked if the other would want to be cloned and what would we want our clone to do for us?

I jokingly told my husband, "You would probably want yours to listen and talk to me as I ramble each day about everything." He did laugh, but then said, "No, I like listening to you."

He thought I would like my clone to stay behind while I traveled the world. I explained, "No way, it would only be fun if I were doing it WITH you."

Ask yourself this: If I wanted to be cloned to be a better version of myself, what would he/she look like and HOW do I become that? If I wanted to be cloned to take over my life, what do I need to do to start enjoying everything about my life? What am I missing that would make me want to escape my life or change it? What is stopping me from doing it today? Alternatively, what negative things would I have my clone do? Why am I avoiding those tasks or people or situations?

c) **Let's Get It On.** Yes, I will be discussing sex, so buckle up. Did you know the number one reason men have affairs is due to lack of physical affection in their relationship? This is not surprising, but did you know there is a much deeper reason than just S. E. X.? It is the connection, the acceptance, and the closeness needed to feel respected and, yes, loved. For men, it is a need to feel wanted, sexually desired, and to feed the ego. The ability to please a woman physically goes back to the caveman ideation of providing and sustaining the household and family.

Couples always need to maintain intimacy in a relationship. If one partner is lacking the "want," one or both partners need to dig in and find out why. Are there health issues? Tired from work, kids, life? Offer to help. Start practicing some meditation to release tension. Invest time and energy into intimacy and the importance of having intimacy within the relationship. Rekindle the spark, create spontaneous new ideas for outings (and innings in the bedroom).

One night, my husband and I were having a great conversation post-intimate encounter. We had just recovered from the holidays and the business of getting back to our normal routines. I realized it had been quite a while since we had time alone together to get intimately reconnected, but I also realized it had not affected our relationship in any way. I looked back at past relationships and recalled how guilty and insecure those partners had been if we weren't having intercourse constantly.

I mentioned to my husband how great it is that we don't measure the health of our relationship based on the number of times we engage in intercourse. He also had the same experiences with others in the past. Then I said something profound…99 percent of seduction happens outside of the bedroom.

Read that again.

I felt so secure and loved regardless of the "act" and how many times it was or was not happening. I told Dennis, "You make me feel so loved, cared for, and affirmed that sex is just an ingredient in our recipe and not the main course."

Have you ever been in the counting game with a partner? Been guilted by your lack of giving your body to someone? Felt obligated, if I get this done, he/she will do what I need? If this is the case in your current affair, re-evaluate how you are valued outside of the relationship bedroom.

d) **The buck stops here.** How much integration of finances is there in your marriage? How much openness and trust is there in your financial life together? Money and finances can be areas of contention, anxiety, secrets, shame, etc. Our relationship with money is VERY programmed from our upbringing and childhood. If you came from a home with very frugal parents, you see money as a limited commodity. If you came from a wealthy home, you may not have any idea what a budget is. Or if you had previous relationships where others took advantage or even stole money from you, it would establish mistrust on the money front. Unfortunately, there is a weird stigma and shame when it comes to money. People sometimes feel uncomfortable discussing it when dating, before marriage, and even after marriage.

I had one such trigger when my husband and I were engaged. In my past, I never let anyone complete my taxes or pay my bills, and I mean since I started working at fifteen years old. In every relationship I have had, I was in charge of the money task.

My husband asked if he could prepare our joint tax forms once we were married, and I panicked!

I had a previous relationship that was long term, six years long, and this person had an alcohol and gambling addiction. He was unemployed and I carried the burden of paying for all the household bills. He would steal my debit card out of my purse (we had separate accounts) and run my account into the negative. I would put a lock on my purse (yes, that is a very unhealthy mind-set, I know) so that he would not be able to take my card and fraudulently spend MY money.

You can see how difficult it was for me to let go of some of those fears and control about finances when I met my husband. It was a huge leap of trust to even let him pay our mutual bills. I can say that it was crucial to let go of this view in order to have a healthy and honest relationship with my husband.

He was very patient, and I would definitely credit him for helping me overcome my fear and mistrust related to relationships and finances. More specifically, he helped me release the feeling that I would lose everything I worked so hard for if I relinquished control.

He created a spreadsheet, and he was (as was I) transparent about income, expenses, savings, life insurance, 401(k), etc.

Phew!

That was so difficult for me, but now, I trust him implicitly with our financial future. So much so, I have no idea most of the time what's in our joint account, but that's how much I trust now. I maintained my independence by keeping a separate account for business expenses and savings.

Just do it!

Have the talk. Be open, be honest, and plan together. When viewed as a team, it is more exciting to budget or save for a mutual goal.

If you and your partner are uneasy about having "the money talk," ease into it by suggesting a list of all the household bills and expenses.

Consider this to be similar to journaling; once you put something on paper it doesn't seem so ominous.

When my daughter Jordan moved in with her boyfriend, finances was an area she was very uncomfortable discussing. You just dive in and see where your level of comfort ends. They were able to find a great solution that worked for them. A joint account for household bills, a joint savings for their future goals, and separate accounts for a portion of their own spending desires.

The fact that they discovered this equation in the early stage of the relationship is so healthy! She called me and told me how she felt a weight was lifted and that it felt more like a partnership now that it was addressed.

If you wait to discuss these things until you are already intertwined in leases, cars, or phone plans, it just compounds the problem. It ties back to trust and having the need to discuss complicated co-mingled finances and is more difficult than starting with a joint checking account and establishing transparency early in the relationship.

Remember that sacrifices and compromises must be made. In most couples, there is a saver and there is a spender. Allowing the saver to have a set amount for security eliminates stress. Allowing the spender to have a set amount creates freedom. Resentments can build if there is not a good balance for each partner, just like every other area of the relationship. As the partnership progresses, situations will arise where these conversations will need to continue. For instance, if you start out renting an apartment together, how you will move to home ownership will be an area to discuss.

My husband is very generous about spending while I am a little more cautious. This is certainly due to our past experiences with money. As a single-parent, single-income household, I was conditioned to only spend on the necessities for survival. Even now when I spend money on something a little frivolous, I carry a certain amount of guilt and feel the need to explain to Dennis what a bargain I got, or why I really desired the purchase. His response is usually "You don't have explain it to me, and I don't need to know how much you saved. It's okay." I love his understanding and generosity, and it is my issue to let go of past programming.

Moving further, when it comes to renovating our home, I hate spending large amounts on things. If they aren't broken, why spend money to replace them? One example was when my husband wanted all new windows in our home. Fancy, double-paned, energy efficient windows. Ugh! I felt like the windows were fine, I could see out of them, and they kept us dry. What more did we need? That is such a Mars versus Venus difference of thinking, I know. Luckily, my husband is patient and he walked me through the need for the new windows. He didn't get mad or lecture (he is an engineer after all) on all of the reasons the current windows were old and failing—some leaked, and we could save money on our power bill.

I love this about him, and it is a great way to communicate without condescension.

It is very important that a couple addresses each situation separately as it comes up. Many times, the spender

and the saver will make blanket statements like "You
always want to spend money on..." or "Why don't I ever
get to buy what I want?" Communicate your needs and
try not to generalize about spending.

Chapter 2

SWIPE TO THE LEFT, LET'S TALK DATING

One of the challenges in relationships is the HOW of finding a partner. This chapter could fill the entire book, but let's get right to it.

An online article[1] by Kendra Cherry, who has a Master of Science degree in educational psychology, states that psychologist Zick Rubin proposed romantic love is made up of three elements:

1. Attachment

2. Caring

3. Intimacy

Rubin believed that sometimes we experience a great amount of appreciation and admiration for others. We enjoy spending time with them and want to be around them, but this does not necessarily qualify as love. Instead, Rubin referred to this as liking.

---

[1]   https://www.verywellmind.com/theories-of-love-2795341

Love, on the other hand, is much deeper, more intense, and includes a strong desire for physical intimacy and contact. People who are "in like" enjoy each other's company, while those who are "in love" care as much about the other person's needs as they do their own.

What comes along with dating and the process of finding your "person," unfortunately, is the arduous task of healing old wounds and viewing yourself with the highest regard.

There are many dating rituals within modern society, and they have changed over time. Unless you live in a cave hidden away from all humanity, you know that currently, online dating is the prevalent path to finding "the one."

To be successful in the journey of finding our perfect partner, we must first look at ourselves and take inventory of what we offer.

Jade, my chihuahua, is a little overweight, so we call her Waddles or Fat Baby. This is endearing and I hardly think she minds. However, when she walks up the stairs to our room, we cannot watch her. If she sees us watching her climb, she turns around and goes back down. She is self-conscious about how slow or scared she is. I am assuming, of course, since she hasn't disclosed her reasons.

We all have insecurities, but do we let them control our actions or inactions of searching for love? How do you view yourself? Are you using the scope of others or your past? Make a list of your attributes and assets. Read it every day until it sinks into your subconscious and creates the new view of yourself you want to be.

I have a short exercise for my clients that has been quite effective:

1. I ask the client to make a list of three people they admire (it can be historical figures, celebrities, family, dead or alive).

2. I then ask them to list the qualities or characteristics they admire about the three people.

3. I then instruct them to wake up in the morning, visualize the qualities sewn into a jacket, cape, shirt, whatever is preferable, and to put it on. This gives them the sense that they are and have those qualities. It's a confidence-building technique and a see-it-before-it-happens method of boosting our positive perspective of ourselves.

To help you understand my perspective on relationships, here is a little background on my relationship past life and why my life experiences give me the reference material to speak on a broad range of relationships. I have been married twice. I have also had long-term relationships and lots of dating relationships in between. You could say I was unknowingly doing a lot of research for this book and career that one day would come to pass. I met my husband on an online dating site; therefore, I do know that it can work. I had to kiss a lot of frogs (more than I care to disclose here) before finally meeting my prince.

I also had to take time off from dating to heal from previous hurts and betrayals and really look at what I was doing in those relationships. I had to answer (for myself) why I was settling for *barely good enough*, and what was I lacking that I was trying to fill with the love from someone else.

Phew!

It was hard, lonely, shameful, and amazing! However, when I "did the work" of learning about myself, it became so clear that I was worthy of the love I unconditionally give. Then, I attracted exactly what I needed at the level I had healed to. Within the Law of Attraction, like attracts like; that which onto itself is drawn will match at your energy level. It's that simple. Says me, right?

I remember calling my best friend, Linda, after another unsuccessful first date. I was so excited as I exclaimed after she asked how it went, "It was great! He was a total narcissist and self-involved!" She was confused by my enthusiasm. "No, it was great because for the first time ever, I recognized the signs and red flags and said, 'No, thank you.'"

It really was a revelation for me since I was always baffled at my lack of discernment at the start of these dysfunctional relationships. Even if you have gone on 100 dates and still haven't connected with your soul mate, just think of all the sorting you are doing. You are getting so much clarity about what you really want! If someone checks some of the boxes, most of the boxes, or none of the boxes, keep going. Examine how you are screening your emails and conversations. Look critically at how you are selecting the person you are thinking about having in your life.

One of the reasons I find our furry pets are so much more content than we are is their ability to know immediately if they like someone. When an unfamiliar visitor comes to your home, do you notice how your dogs either go right to them with a wagging tail or stay by your side for protection? Brodie is the best judge of character, Jade, not so much as she likes everyone. It is as if Brodie has a sixth sense and feels energy before a person even speaks. When my best girlfriend, Linda, comes over for coffee, Brodie always goes to his toy box and brings her a baby. My granddog, Callie, is very specific when greeting men. She either jumps all over them or barks her little head off from a distance. It can be somewhat embarrassing to my daughter as she tries to explain Callie's behavior (or tries to excuse it) without offending the person. What's even more interesting is you cannot convince these animals to accept something they feel isn't right. Talk about staying true to themselves!

When it comes to online dating, the key is to be honest—brutally honest. Statistics state that the most common denominator on profiles is this: Men most often lie about their height, and women most frequently lie about their weight. Sadly, the expectations of others tend to create these lies. It's harmless in some ways, but unfortunately, if we cannot tell the truth about our physical facts, how will we ever get to the root of being truthful about our most intimate thoughts, dreams, needs, and desires?

My husband, Dennis, reached out to me on a dating site and piqued my interest right away. He was funny, a straight shooter, and very intelligent. Sounds like I should have immediately set up a date, right? Well, I didn't. I was still adamant about healing and, truth be told, not willing to go out into the dating arena just yet. I told him I was just looking for a friend... hmmm, on a dating site?

In fact, we corresponded for four months and I still declined to go out with him—yet. Please don't get me wrong; he was not pushy at all. Very subtle and gentlemanly. He would send a text every few weeks and ask again if I would like to go out.

One day, while sitting at my desk on a Wednesday morning, I received a text from him stating, "How about that dinner date?" I thought, *This guy is persistent and classy,* so I said yes.

Even when I first met him and spoke to him at that initial date, I was somewhat self-sabotaging, or at least being very cautious and probably feeling a little fear of the unknown. I blatantly stated, "You should update your profile picture; you look older than your picture." I also stated, "I thought you'd be taller." I realize now that I reflect upon it how rude that was, and the fact that he stayed and gave me a shot is a miracle. It is safe to say most women would have been highly offended by such comments.

As it turns out, he never sent the text I received, or at least he didn't send it on that particular day. (Divine universal intervention possibly?) We still haven't figured out how it happened, but we met for that wonderful first date that ended up being six hours long and a genuine, fun connection. I had this awesome realization that I had finally healed and attracted a similar spirit who met the needs and desires I had set for myself. I wasn't repeating the insanity cycle I had perpetuated for most of my adult life!

The best thing I ever did for myself was to learn to like myself. I mean I learned to like being with me, doing things alone, building my self-esteem, and changing my self-talk, self-thought, and beliefs about what I was worth. When you reach this point, you will find it so empowering, and the choices in front of you become so clear on which way to go. You will find a renewed hope that you will meet the perfect mate for you. You will then trust your judgment and know that you will stick to only what is good and serves your soul best.

Are you ready?

Here are some questions to ask yourself if you are starting the pursuit of finding your lifetime love:

1. **Do I have the time to invest?** Will you take time to correspond over time, meet up with suitors, talk on the phone, text as warranted? If you answered no, then stop and remove yourself from the process. Here's an analogy: If your keys are lost and you only look for them every now and then, you may never find them. But if the keys are still lost, and you really want to go for a drive in your car, do you expect them to just appear when you're sitting in the driver's seat? Dating is a commitment. It takes energy, time, and effort. This isn't to say you need spend all of your waking hours online and juggling fifteen different people, but you have to look deep within yourself and say, "Am I willing to take the time to figure it out?"

My best friend used to tell me dating was a hobby for me. Yes, it was. However, I only put my energy into those I felt were a good fit. If a phone call gave me indications of anything below my bar, I would not move forward to a date. If a date showed me our chemistry and intellect were not a match, I would not move forward. I used to have the mantra "I don't owe anybody anything, and my time and energy are valuable."

Do not be afraid to speak your truth and say, "I don't think we are a good fit." You will know from the start if something just clicks. It's best to be honest from the beginning. If you are unsure, it's okay to give it another try. Just don't be blind or overlook issues or behaviors that make you uncomfortable, and don't make excuses for anything that rubs you the wrong way or feels off.

2. **Do I think about a past relationship in anger or sadness?** If the answer is yes, then hold off on dating. You have some healing to do still. Try a Reiki session or meditation for release. Pray for gratitude for the person and experience. Until you heal this part, you will be seeking as well as attracting the same person, different face, and comparing everyone to the last one. When you get to the place of contentment related to the past, and have an enthusiasm for the future, you will then be open to something new.

3. **Am I committed to see the truth and not what I want it to be?** Many of my single friends tend to make excuses for someone who is a "nice" person. They are basically saying, "He has one thing out of twenty on my checklist, and that makes him good enough." They don't see exactly what's in front of them, the other nineteen criteria that are NOT being met. Or they say he has everything they want but has issues he needs to fix. Um, his issues are what will not allow the relationship to succeed. His issues are the dealbreakers.

For example, he's a good person but he has commitment phobia.

I hear this often: "I think he was nervous; he probably doesn't act like that normally." (Um, he probably does.)

"I want to give him (or her) the benefit of the doubt." (Why? Has he earned this?)

"I'll give them more chances." (Again, you don't owe anyone extra time to convince you that they are the one for you.)

I often say, "Don't waste your makeup, girl." Meaning, don't spend time or energy when you are already being nudged by your intuition to let it go.

We call these red flags. My daughter Lacee has a saying: "Don't put the red flags in your bag." In other words, don't overlook something and think it will go away. This is not *Let's Make a Deal*. It's your life and your search for your true love.

The ideal someone is a person who is in control of their emotions, who speaks eloquently and handles themselves with class regardless of the external circumstance. They will resonate with you on all levels. They will have the traits, characteristics, and morals you desire. Don't make excuses for anyone; see it for what it is.

I find through my friends, my coaching clients, and my own experience, the greater the suffering from past hurt, the more we tend to disregard the warning signs because a new relationship still offers something better than the last failed relationship.

My first marriage was a dysfunctional and abusive relationship. When I met my second husband, the bar was NOT very high; "just don't abuse me" was my hope. Although he was a great person, I look back now and realize I hadn't set expectations of what I really deserved and needed. I did not spend enough time healing from the damage caused by my first husband, so here was a new prospective relationship that didn't have to face a specific checklist. I loved him as a person and the kindness he showed me, but the deeper connection I needed for myself as well as my children wasn't there. This is how we accept and settle for a less than desirable relationship. We would be better friends than partners. I just didn't understand or discern the difference at the time.

When a stray dog has been recovered and taken to the shelter, staff will perform an aggression test. This is to see how a dog behaves around other dogs, as well as whether the new dog attempts to reach for another dog's food when eating. If they show aggression, staff tries to work with them, but many times the dog can never overcome the learned aggression and therefore is unable to be adopted. Like these dogs, the aggression is a red flag. Staff knows it is something that is innately programmed and may not be overcome. In the same way, we should do our own aggression test, or at least a characteristic test. We need to accept the results of our test, and if the core poor or unacceptable behavior is significant enough to us, then we should move on to the next candidate and not try to "fix" this person.

4. **Am I a good catch**? If you do not have full confidence in who you are and what you bring to the dating table, then postpone dating life. This is not a tit for tat where you measure his/her shortcomings with your own. Example: "Well, my credit is not good, so it's okay that he's forty and lives with his mom." What??!!

When I hear these things, I know that you are not ready to attract the perfect person for you. If you don't view your life and yourself as the best things since sliced bread, you will be making exceptions left and right for others. Be proud of all that you have acquired, achieved, and created up to the point of dating someone.

You earned it, you learned, you lived, you grew! Be proud!

A short story about some of my growth. I was working two jobs, with a daughter in college and a son at home, when the financial upheaval of 2008 happened. As the real estate market declined, it was difficult to handle expenses for the mortgage, help my daughter, and support my son. I got a job serving at a restaurant, in addition to my full-time day job, in the evenings to offset costs and to save my home. At the time, I started dating a man who actually said this, "It's very selfish of you to work two jobs."

I could not believe he said that!

I was striving to keep my home for stability for my teenage son (who needed a consistent routine as he had been clinically diagnosed with ADHD), help my daughter with college expenses, and save everything I had worked for with no assistance whatsoever. I was proud of how solution minded I was and of my diligent work ethic! This person saw it as a negative trait? How much further apart could we have been in our morals, values, and goals?

Those are the signs that we must pay attention to. Needless to say, I am glad I walked away from being devalued in that way, and it will never happen again.

5. **Am I learning from every encounter?** I know it can be frustrating to go on date after date and not find the perfect match. It can feel like a waste of time, but is it? Emphatically I say no! Why? Because you find clarity about what you want in every single encounter you have in the courting world. Imagine if you view it this way now: You are one date closer to your person. Maybe he added DO NOT WANTS to your list, which is good, since now you are even better at seeing signs. Stay positive and see every moment as a chance to learn from someone.

Let's take a moment to reflect on how our animals view the mating process. Most of our furry babies don't really have a mating process; however, we can still emulate the carefree attitude they show toward other creatures such as themselves. They go to the dog park, run around, meet up with other dogs, enjoy their day, and go home with their people. Not too complicated, correct? You will see a scuffle here and there because they just aren't jiving with a specific furry friend, but they move on. We should essentially be that light-hearted about dating.

In my life coaching practice, after doing a lot of internal work about false beliefs and healing from our past, if my client is a single person, we create an avatar of their ideal partner. In creation, it is a vision board of traits they desire in a mate. I ask them to place it in an area where they will see it every day like a bathroom mirror, refrigerator, or in their pocket or purse. It sets the desired outcome or person into our subconscious mind or storage locker of wants. By doing this, they activate the Law of Attraction, and only those at the same level (or vibration) will be brought into their path.

At the end of this book is a sample diagram of that exercise where you can list the features that you require and desire in a perfect mate. I encourage you to take some time to explore this as one of the steps of having your perfect relationship.

By reprogramming what we believe in ourselves, we can obtain the relationship that we desire.

I have seen it work wonders.

One client of mine was struggling with attracting men who met her criteria. After creating an avatar and focusing on those aspects, she started attracting quality men, and her dance card was quickly filled! She learned how to maintain her standards and could easily decide who was a match for what she was looking for. Deeper connections and intellectual conversations began to take precedence over physical appearance and superficial possessions. Even more, I recently received information that she found her match and is exploring moving into a committed phase! I was so excited that she used the tools with success!

I would suggest this to anyone looking to begin the dating process. I would also classify it as "setting your bar." But you must stick to it. Let's look at it this way: When you have a job, your boss doesn't say it's okay to only do some of the tasks you are assigned; you are required to do all of the tasks. Make sure all of your boxes are being marked off in the search for love.

Never make excuses for someone else's behavior or views. If they don't match what you are seeking, then move on. I will keep repeating this: Don't waste your energy on someone you just don't flow with. And your relationship should be that: a flow.

We have all heard that marriage and relationships are "work."

Work indicates something that is hard or something for which you always have to try hard. Until I met my husband, I believed this. I believed the harder maintaining my relationship was, the more reward there was at the end. I thought the arguing was inevitable and would bring us closer and make us stronger.

Nope!

I now see it as practice versus work. You get better with practice.

Arguing just builds resentments, especially when you are consistently putting your needs aside to appease someone else. In a healthy relationship, everything falls into place, we coexist naturally, and we live in peace and harmony. Being married to my ideal partner has shown me that it isn't work; it isn't hard. Our relationship is joyful and easy since we are both at the same level of understanding and unconditional love. We trip over ourselves to make each other happy.

I never knew this was possible. When you've only been loved conditionally, you start to believe that if you give enough, love enough, try enough, they will love you back. The untruth of this is so apparent, but not until you've been loved the way you love. That is the key—"to be loved the way that I love."

That is the goal.

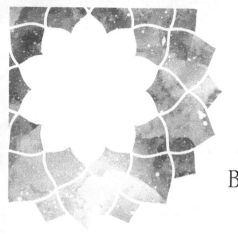

Chapter 3

BUT I FEEL SUCH A CONNECTION

Let's expand on the dating and evolution of a relationship. First, inventory what you bring to a relationship:

What are your best qualities?

How about your worst?

What are your fears?

Your triggers?

What are your goals (financial, family, exercise, etc.)?

Are you committed to giving your time?

Then examine what your needs and requirements are for your ideal partner:

Are you expecting more than you want to give?

Do you want to be treated like a queen and feel your potential mate should bow down?

Where do you envision your partner to be in their life (financial, employment, children, etc.)?

The understanding of your needs and requirements for your "forever" partner is critical to understanding yourself.

As Brodie and Jade are fairly confined to the borders of our house and backyard, you would think they have every inch memorized. One day while observing them, I saw something interesting. They went around the backyard sniffing and listening to the sounds of our suburban neighborhood and their fellow dog neighbors. Jade, our chihuahua, discovered something, a rock, a bug, a buried bone (who knows?) and Brodie ran over to check it out.

She brought a new awareness to what would be a normal and mundane day in the yard. In this same way, what are you bringing that is new and exciting to your partnership? Are you spontaneous? Creative? My favorite thing to do is surprise my husband with something unexpected. He loves that I do this. Recently, I bought tickets to a concert to a band that he didn't know was in town. He didn't know which we were attending until we were at the venue. He missed the billboard as we were driving to the venue, so it wasn't until we were in line that I disclosed the band. It adds this ingredient of excitement and fun to the relationship.

If we are in a relationship that is not fulfilling, we must look within ourselves and determine if we are giving what we expect in return. There's an old saying, "To have a friend, you must be a friend." This pertains directly to our romantic relationships as well.

Are you providing love, encouragement, and understanding? Or are you critical, condescending, and find fault in others? As I mentioned in my previous book, **My Dog Is More**

Enlightened Than I Am, if you are looking for something, you will find it, whether negative or positive. It is all in your perspective and what you are focused on.

When you think about the ideal mate, be sure you are introspective about your own ability to give fully to exploring new opportunities. There is no one on the planet who can fill a void, provide confidence, security, and well-being as a substitute for you doing those things for yourself.

I speak often to people who are in the dating realm and navigating the process. When questioned about what they are seeking, they commonly say, "I don't know." Most often I'll get this checklist of physical characteristics or even the monetary and perfunctory job and car requirements. I think it's hard to put into words the connection and emotions we seek from another. It's best to use scenarios such as "If I am sick, will they bring me soup?" "If I were to lose a family member, will they be a rock of emotional support?" "On my worst day, will they be patient or run screaming for the hills?" Just the screening process is toiling let alone the bumps along the road of relationship growth.

In this new age of electronic meetups, here are some interesting terms that have been designated about the status of a dating relationship according to some online sites.

Kittenfishing is a little like catfishing, but while catfishing is more about wholly <u>misrepresenting yourself</u>, kittenfishing is a little less serious. Think of it as stretching the truth a little bit but not egregiously.

Breadcrumbing: That is, they keep throwing little bits out there to keep the other person thinking that they might have a shot at a date or relationship. They don't throw out too many breadcrumbs to the point they have to agree to go out with the person—they throw out just enough to keep the person around.

Cushioning: When you're in a relationship, but you aren't sure if it's going to last, you start chatting with other people and stringing them along. That way, if you <u>break up with your partner</u>, you'll have other options to cushion your fall.

Three and Out: After three months of dating, which is about enough time for <u>the honeymoon period</u> to wear off and people's true colors to start shining through, people usually decide whether to continue or to break up.

Vampiring: Going out with someone, usually in the same field of work, to see if you can suck contacts or job prospects from them. This is also known as "a milk date," where you're milking the person for recommendations, advice, or connections. It's considered an easy (and unethical) way of trying to get your foot in the door in a chosen industry.

Ghosting: You meet someone, you go on a date, you have a great time. You text back and forth. Then, one day, you send them a text and don't get a response. You wait a few days. You figure they are probably just busy. Then weeks go by and you realize that whatever you had is over as they appear to have fallen off the planet.

Orbiting: This is a new, terrible trend in dating. In orbiting, a person will ghost you, but continue to stalk your social media. You wouldn't know this is happening with Facebook or Twitter, but Instagram stories and Snapchat tell you which users have watched your content.

Firedooring: This is when one person has all of the power in an exchange. Someone who will text you but fail to respond when you text back. Someone who will never make plans to see you but expect you to drop everything and come over when they happen to have an afternoon free. As the name implies, this is not a two-way street. It's a fire door, which is a one-way exit. You can get out, but you can't get back in.

Situationship: Circling back to the fact that everyone these days is wildly commitment-phobic, a "situationship" is a sexual relationship that stops short of being a committed relationship. You're together but you're not *together* together. You're in a situation.

Stashing: You're dating someone, and you feel like it's going well. But you notice that they don't feature you in any of their social media, or they detag themselves from posts you put up. This is the modern version of getting weird when you ask to meet your partner's parents. The person you're with is into you, but they aren't sure they want to close the door on other possibilities, and therefore "stash you" as one would with a basket of dirty laundry, in the closet.

One and done: This is exactly as it sounds. You have one date or sexual experience and the relationship is done. Or one last fling before ending a relationship.

Texting buddy: This one is probably more common for the mature daters. It's when you've connected online, give your phone number, and then it's an endless texting saga. They want to be in contact, but don't ask you out.

Uber Radius: Determining someone's desirability based on the distance between where he/she lives and where you live.

There are other definitions relating to sexual preferences and dating which we will address in upcoming chapters.

Unbelievably, this is not all-inclusive of the labels. Phew! How does anyone find the one in these current times? The funny part is that the behavior hasn't changed much over the centuries, only the names and technology involved. I think there is so much information overload that we may end up skeptical and cautious of anyone who approaches us. Plus, for many women, when they are online dating, the choices are overwhelming. There are too many people approaching you, and those approaches vary from way too aggressive to far too passive. It is almost impossible to differentiate between good and bad and to give someone enough respect to even be considered for that first date is almost impossible.

In the case of too many choices, a common mistake (or ploy in some cases) is that we seek this specific connection where we only need a solitary "sign" that a person could be our soulmate. This makes the selection process easier (and quicker), but it's a trap that keeps us away from our soulmate. We are not focused on the full spectrum of our needs, only on a superficial quality or item that speaks to us.

The sign could be mentioning a song they love that is meaningful to you as well. It could be a family dynamic. "I was raised by a single mom, so I really respect you for that." It could be a romantic fantasy such as "I want to look across the room at someone and know what they are thinking or share a secret without even speaking." I'm giving an eyeroll, because I fell for this one at one point. Even something as simple as sharing a favorite food, color, or travel destination is not enough to know if you could spend the remainder of your days with them.

Do any of those sound familiar?

With the technology today, love seekers have gotten very good at their taglines. Long gone are the corny lines about long walks on beaches. Due to the quantity (not necessarily the quality) of people you swim through in your online dating email ocean, you have subconsciously homed in on what grabs your attention.

Unfortunately, some serial daters know what the trigger points are, and have the ability to at least cajole you to crack open the dating door. The dilemma with this is that you can falsely believe it was meant to be because a sign was there. The conundrum is that you can't be naïve, and at the same time you can't be overly skeptical either. The true test is listening not just to what they say to you, but what they don't say.

Be observant of their actions, not just their words.

I recall a date I went on where we met for dinner. When the waiter walked away, my date complained about the waiter's lack of service or attentiveness. I didn't see it. I saw a hardworking individual doing their best. That was a very good indicator that we didn't have the same perspective or core values.

Unless you physically meet with a person, spend time with them, and really find out who they are, you can't assume they are a good match. The only surefire way to know is to spend at least all four seasons, twelve months of a year, together, and witness someone in everyday situations such as at work or with their family and friends. Don't take a shortcut. See everything with open eyes and ears. Being in love with being in love can convolute the waters of mate finding.

Chapter 4

WE ARE A FAMILY

As I was finishing up this book, I recognized that I had been coaching clients and receiving calls related to a subject I hadn't addressed: Family Issues.

I thought it would be remiss of me to exclude this content as it plays a huge part in relationships.

Although we like to believe a relationship consists of two people, it also includes the family and friends of your potential partner and yourself. This can cause quite a bit of conflict and we need to insert boundaries.

When my daughter came to live with me as an adult, she also brought Callie, her dog. I was a little worried about adding another energetic dog to my peaceful two-dog existence. I was careful to observe their interactions and help them blend their dog pack. Interestingly enough, it was no problem. My dogs have been socializing at dog parks since they were puppies and welcome new visitors, thank goodness. What I noticed was the tolerance that each had for one another right from the start. As it evolved, it became even better as they adapted to one another, especially Callie with her overabundance of border collie energy. Jade would play and roughhouse with Callie even though she wasn't used to doing so with her brother Brodie. I love that dogs accept and adjust easily to one another or at least that mine were able to.

When you begin dating someone, as I explained in Chapter 3, it's important to ask crucial questions. Relationships with family are key to knowing what dynamic the person comes from or what the "norm" means to them regarding family interactions. Again, being open and honest would be vital to allow someone to make an educated decision.

There are several cultures, behaviors and dynamics that can be difficult for a couple to overcome when it comes to family. If the couple are determined to put their relationship as a top priority and able to put healthy boundaries in place, these should be small speed bumps rather than mountains to conquer.

1. **Cutting the apron strings:** In this dynamic, the tie between a parent and child may be codependent, some may even say enabling. If an adult child is still asking a parent to pay bills, make decisions, or do tasks a capable adult should be doing, it can cause dissention in the couple as one partner can feel as if they aren't partners and not needed or valued for their contributions. If a parent is financially connected to the partners, it will create a tug-of-war of power and control.

2. **Helicopter parents:** This type of parent/child relationship is where boundaries are desperately needed. When a parent inserts themselves in every aspect of a couple, it can be a control issue or some insecurity

of "losing their baby" to a spouse or romantic partner. The adult child must express their feelings and put boundaries down and stick to them. The difficulty in this is not wanting to hurt the parent's feelings. It can be done with love and respect, but it must be done for a healthy relationship to exist with a romantic partner.

3. **Ongoing dissention:** Most families have some type of issues or conflict. There is no perfect family; after all, we are continuously learning through each stage of life. However, when the conflict in a family carries over to a couple's contentment, it can cause a rift between them. It's hard not to get sucked in to a family's longtime dynamic and drama. Each individual within the couple should consider their couple-hood as a safe island separate from the family. This will establish a team view of unity, and help the couple avoid having family drama get between them.

4. **Childhood carryover:** Not only in relationships, but also in mental health in general, childhood trauma is the number one cause of issues. Carrying the baggage of past trauma from your upbringing will surely break a couple down. If conflict is addressed as blaming the past, it will be a continuing cycle with no resolution. Release work and mindful intentions to let the past go will help you objectively resolve conflicts in the relationship. Sometimes just letting the spouse vent about their family is enough for them to be heard. They need to release the feelings and work through it themselves, but having a supportive mate can be part of the release

work. Try not to judge and do not lecture! Most likely they have been working this through their entire lives and feel they are helpless to control it, so just be empathetic and loving.

5. **Deal or No Deal:** Avoidance of family is not a solution, no matter how tempting it is. The exception being if it's a toxic and abusive state of affairs causing more harm than good by engaging. If a parent(s) comes over unannounced, tells you how to organize your home or your life, dictates how to clean your house, or calls ten times a day, it's time to figure out what is best for your partnership. Holidays are especially difficult to figure out as each family has their own traditions. They may not be okay with changing the expectations of each member.

As a couple, decide how to handle these hurdles. You'll need to compromise. For example: alternate years or holidays. Set the number of times you will see each family per year. It's most important that each spouse is shown respect. It is unacceptable for a family member to disrespect your choice of partner. Communicating and displaying this to your spouse will solidify their respect and trust for you, knowing you value them and their feelings above all else.

6. **Parenting versus Grandparenting:** This one can be a doozy! The issue is more prevalent between moms and daughters and mothers-in-law and daughters-in-law. As a grandma myself, I've learned the joys of grandparenting by just enjoying the fun of the kids. They can have candy, get messy, yell, dance, and sing as

much as they want! I did my parenting duties, and now I get to enjoy the spoils without the responsibilities. Many parents (mostly moms) want to give unsolicited advice to new parents. It can sound like criticism and can lower a new mom's self-confidence. Many moms also think parenting should be done the exact same way they did it. I disagree. Although my daughter tends to do it the same way I did, it's not through my assertion. There is also a chance of conflict when a grandparent does something different from a parent's wishes. Luckily, my daughter and I have learned to agree that "what happens at Grandma's house stays at Grandma's house." It used to drive her crazy early on when she would get my granddaughter all fixed up pretty and I would hand her a cupcake. Give me some credit, she had a bib on, but still, she didn't see it from my perspective. It's important to establish what you want as a parent without being too overwhelming. Grandparents must also respect your wishes regarding your ideas of parenting. I would encourage letting grandparents enjoy the freely given love of their grandchildren with a limited number of rules.

7. **Blended Families:** With the rates of divorce in today's society, when you are dating as an adult, meeting someone with children is highly likely. This is a challenge in so many ways. Not only are you going to have to accept the child(ren), but there is also the potential of co-parenting with your partner's ex-spouse. If the ex has not healed from the hurt of the relationship, they will be inclined to show insecurity and power struggle

when it comes to the children. Be patient. First decide if you are up to the challenge because this is going to bring instances of frustration or insecurity if you let it. Be sure your partner understands the level of respect you want in relation to the ex-partner and children. It needs to be defined long before you are knee deep in commitments.

I am so fortunate and proud of the fact that my husband's ex-spouse, his son's mother, and I get along fabulously. We recently stayed with her and their son for a weekend getaway at her home in the Colorado mountains. It was relaxed and easy and I appreciated the generosity in her to extend the invite. My husband stated on the plane ride home, "This weekend could not have been more enjoyable and I'm so grateful you are kind, and secure enough to spend time with my son and his mom." It wasn't that hard, honestly. I know my worth. I know that my husband is with me because we are a better fit than he was with her. And she is also very secure in her new marriage, so it goes both ways. I also highly respect the healthy co-parenting relationship they have maintained over the years (their son is now twenty-four).

Coparenting and relieving past feelings from a past relationship takes communication and compassion from all parties involved and that can be an goal that with time can be achieved.

Chapter 5

LET'S FACETIME

When I say "facetime," I'm referring to face-to-face meetings, not the video chat communication.

My daughter Jordan lives in Austin, Texas, and I live in Arizona. We communicate through video to connect better than just a phone call. When my grand dog, Bexley, a border collie, sees the video or hears my voice, she looks at the screen briefly, maybe wags her tail, but walks away. When I visit my daughter, Bexley cannot get enough of my attention. She is constantly bringing me her ball, sleeping next to me, or enjoying our walks. The connection is so much deeper when we are in physical contact with one another.

I know it seems that person-to-person conversation with others is almost a lost art, but there are many opportunities for these types of encounters. Meaningful relationships cannot be built solely on texts or emails. I also think that the creation of the Meetup groups was helpful in regenerating the person-to-person meeting with others who share your interests.

At one point, when I was dating after my divorce, I recall being approached by a business that charged a fee for a monthly membership and organized events that singles could attend. I didn't join but I can appreciate the concept, especially for the shy or non-social daters who need some assistance in getting started, or even meeting someone in the first place.

My parents once said to me, in my dating phase, "Why can't you meet someone offline? You're going to get murdered!" Okay, they are of the boomer generation mind-set and I get it that today's technology and methods are unconventional. It is beyond their comprehension how this new stuff works, or how you would find a connection through just a photo and some emails. There has been a generational change with streamlined processes. My reply to them at the time was this: "Would you like me to troll the aisles of Home Depot?" They said "yes." (Eyeroll given at the time.)

So how DO you meet authentically in society today? Some possibilities:

Parties

Networking Events

Organized Meetups

Book Clubs

Hobby Clubs

Yoga

Gym

Work Events

Or anywhere that is a place of interest to you...and yes, it is possible to meet someone by bumping into them at the grocery store or coffee shop, but there is a fine line between being creepy and being engaging. A common interest (books or hobbies or yoga) can evolve naturally into interest into each other.

I was sitting with my friend at Starbucks one day, and a gentleman walked up to me and said, "This may sound weird, but I've noticed you for quite some time. I think you are beautiful and I would love to take you out." I took down his number and thanked him just for the fact that he was confident and bold enough to approach me in an old-fashioned and genuine way. We did go out to dinner once and I thoroughly enjoyed his company. He was a genuinely nice guy (it was raining as we went to our cars and he put his coat over my head when we went out—brownie points for that). We weren't a perfect match, but I appreciated the moment. Sadly, in today's reality we have to be so careful about safety that it has greatly diminished these authentic approaches.

Don't go seeking a hookup and romantic relationship; people can smell desperation a mile away. Unless you want a friend with benefits type of interaction with no strings attached, set your mind-set to make friends and enjoy the company of others. It will authentically present itself depending on your openness to others.

I had an epiphany while speaking to my friend on the phone one day regarding her most recent date-bomb from the night before.

I was explaining to her about the Law of Attraction and that my belief is we are all at a vibration or energetic level. I went on to say, "Wouldn't it be great if our vibration had a color?" Let's have some fun with this. Imagine there are ten colors each associated with ten vibration levels. Vibration levels are determined by these factors:

1. The amount of experience a person has had in their life with pain, joy, overcoming issues, sadness, or emotional intelligence

2. The level of confidence, self-love, self-esteem, and mind-set

3. Beliefs, morals, and spiritual beliefs

4. Intelligence

5. Social skills

If your vibration level was more visible, you could walk into a party or gathering of 100 people and see a rainbow of colors throughout the room surrounding each person. You could look into a mirror and see that you are cloaked in green. As you make your way around the room, you speak to each person and realize that those also enveloped in green have migrated to you and vice versa. You enjoy their conversation, and you are each engaged in the others' knowledge and stories. You've never enjoyed an evening out more than this moment.

In a perfect world, it would be great to KNOW who your people are. Those who are like-minded and relatable, those who resonate with you. This is a reality except the colors are invisible.

The saying that "we just vibe" is not too far-fetched. In essence, when you are at the same vibrational energy, it just works and flows with someone. If we pay attention more to how we are feeling another's energy and follow our gut instinct about those we meet, we will be able to distinguish those who are best suited for us.

I've observed my dogs' instincts so many times and it still fascinates me how they lie next to each other when one feels ill. Or during a walk they'll avoid certain humans or animals yet approach others, all while they are all strangers to them. The way they bark at a stranger at the door but not at a family member even with the door closed. I had written on a dating profile at one time, "If my dog doesn't like you, I probably won't either." Dogs just know. They are like kids in their pureness and ability to feel energy.

Let's review how our perceptions and preconceived beliefs affect our view of dating and relationships.

I attended a seminar this year that talked about how our brains develop and affect our self-image. It was said that in the first part of our lives (from birth to six years old), our subconscious is predominant. The subconscious accepts and stores all of the information and experiences we witness. After age six, it is believed that a person is established in who they are. I do not believe this. I believe that after age six, the conscious mind and inner self allow for rejecting information that doesn't fit our self-image or belief of who we came to be and inherently who our souls really are.

The nature versus nurture controversy will always be a question to me. Exposure to life and its events is our experience and what forms our beliefs.

Let's connect it to romantic relationships. For example: If you witnessed a healthy marriage or relationship, you will be more apt to seek a similar experience because it felt good to be around that exposure. If you seek a partner, you will be most likely to attract others who have experienced, understand, or desire the same level of healthy relationship.

Of course, on the flipside, if you have only witnessed hardship and pain related to relationships, you most likely will attract relationships that teach you by the experience of what doesn't feel good or doesn't bring you the highest joy. Only until you realize (by discovering what we don't want, we also create what we do want) what you truly desire and actionably will pursue.

Here's an interesting concept to contemplate.

I was recently watching a Netflix series titled *Black Mirror*. The episode I was watching was described by The Cut:

https://www.thecut.com/2017/12/black-mirror-season-four-dating-episode-hang-the-dj.html

> "Hang the DJ," from *Black Mirror*'s fourth season on Netflix, introduces Spiro Date, an app that promises to lead you to your perfect match. It is like an optimized Tinder: Instead of relying on humans to select matches, Spiro does it for them. In a calm, Alexa-like voice, Spiro analyzes users' preferences and sets them up on blind dates. Spiro determines who meets, where they meet, what they order for dinner, and how long the relationship will last (12 hours, one year, a lifetime, etc.). We see how it works for the episode's two protagonists, Amy (Georgina Campbell) and Frank (Joe Cole).
>
> Honestly, it seems ideal: a technology that eliminates human error, and promises, after a series of dates,

that you *will* find your one true match and live happily ever after. What a nice (and seemingly untrustworthy) guarantee!

Naturally, Spiro quickly begins to seem both a little bit sinister—notice the guards that oversee dates—and inaccurate in its selections. Frank and Amy forge an instant connection but are only allotted 12 hours together. After they part ways, we get to see how the system continues to unfold. Amy dates a handsome guy for a few months, and then has a string of one-night stands while still thinking of Frank. (Okay, just like real life.) Frank enters into a long-term relationship with a woman who hates him, and he still thinks about Amy. (How is this different from how our selection process is?) Unfortunately, both of them are stuck trusting a dating algorithm.

The interesting premise of this episode is that with all of the technology, they still had to rely on the way they FEEL and the vibration or flow of how it was differentiating each person they went on a date with. There was a lot of questioning the process when the person seemed to be a poor match to the daters' preferences. Haven't we all questioned ourselves while across the dinner table on a first date, and we KNEW within five minutes that this person was not a good fit for us? Did you beat yourself up or question why God/Universe/Life would let this person cross paths with you?

In this episode, the other aspect of Spiro Date is that both parties must agree not to view the "expiration" date of the relationship. When the main character betrays the promise not to look, it messes everything up and reduces the time together to hours, regardless of the original amount of time that they were "supposed" to have together.

Let me ask you this. If you look back on your life's moments, if you had your own "Spiro" that gave you a heads-up about the expiration date of certain relationships, would you want that? If so, what benefit would it have provided? I like the un-knowing, the surprise, the fun that comes along with mystery. The mystery is a part of why humans love roller coasters, surprise parties, competitions, and coincidences (synchronicities).

We love the fun of not knowing the end. No one skips to the end of a book without reading the beginning, or only watches the last five minutes of a movie. We really don't want to know, no matter how much we think we do. We are here to live each moment to the fullest and participate in the learning and fun of life.

If you knew you only had twelve hours with someone, do you think you would give it all you have? Compare this to if you had to be with someone for twenty years; you would probably try to be much more open-minded and giving at that first date.

That's the beauty of not knowing! Every encounter is a big question mark on time length. It could be applied to everything in our lives. Would you stay at a job that you knew would only be temporary? Would you give it your all each and every day?

Why do we need guarantees or promises? That's where we tend to go wrong. In relationships, we crave a degree of certainty. We seek a specific title or label, oftentimes prematurely, so we can peek at the timeline of the experience. The terms "exclusive, committed, engaged, significant other" all come from this human need to know how important and valuable we are to someone. In addition, the programming of generations has sent a false belief message, "I'm alone, there must be something wrong with me." On the contrary, there is something so right about a confident, independent person who loves being alone with themselves.

Searching for someone to share and enhance our lives is what the desire should be rather than the thought that you need someone to complete the voids and insecurities you have about being alone. And further, that you need a partner to show others you are lovable. A partner is not a validation of your worth; it is your choice to add to the already fulfilled life you have created. However, sometimes our desires outstrip our growth and we are anxious to have a relationship when we are not ready for one.

Chapter 6

HEALTHY OR UNHEALTHY, YOU DECIDE

Just as we know the love that grows from living with a dog from the time that it is a puppy, to its adulthood, to its passing, we also experience joy by having known the dog through all phases of its life.

In the right long-term relationship, we can also find the joy of knowing someone, and being known BY someone, throughout the phases of our life. This is one of the things that we seek in our human bond and relationships: the growing, changing, and adapting through acceptance and love for one another over time.

This chapter is for the long-timers—those of you who have been in long-term relationships and marriage for quite some time.

My parents have been together since they were seventeen years old and married when they were nineteen years old. They have been together now for fifty-three years! While longevity is meaningful, I have only seen a handful of couples who grew together throughout the years.

Let's examine how couples grow together:

1. We love spending time together, whether a quiet night at home or a night on the town.

2. We have children together and parent as a team.

3. We have the same goals, dreams, and morals.

4. They "get" me—in other words, they love all of my quirks or habits.

5. They fulfill my needs and wants.

6. They make me a better person.

7. They are financially, emotionally, mentally, and spiritually supportive and compatible.

8. They are not just my spouse; they are my friend.

9. They enjoy and endure the ups and downs of life with me.

10. They are my partner in everything from chores to life decisions.

11. They love and respect me.

12. They allow me freedom, space, independence, and the ability to be an individual.

13. They are unconditional in their love for me, and they put my happiness as a priority.

I recently completed certification in a course titled "7 Step Recovery from Infidelity for Couples" and found the below statements would, in fact, lead to a breakdown in committed, long-term couples and often cause infidelity.

Now let's clarify these for couples who remain in relationships that are not healthy:

1. I am expected to always be <u>where</u> my spouse wants me to be. Controlling behavior is disguised as caring and concern.

2. I'll wait until the children are grown and see if we still make it.

3. They don't support what I want to do, my interests, my dreams. They are not engaged in conversations that matter to me.

4. They constantly nag me about my faults.

5. It feels like my needs aren't met, that my spouse doesn't care about my feelings.

6. We never have sex. I'm not interested in being intimate with my spouse.

7. I have to support my spouse's well-being. I financially take care of the family.

8. I don't even like my spouse, even though I may love them.

9. When anything happens, it's my fault. We don't communicate at all and play the blame game continuously.

10. The balance of the responsibilities within our home and our life together are not even.

11. I do not feel loved or respected by my spouse.

12. I feel suffocated.

13. If I do what he/she wants, then they will love me.

There are a multitude of books, classes, retreats, and seminars on relationships and marriage.

There are two crucial areas that must be met in a marriage. Love and Respect.

Yes, I know, we can think of a lot of other areas such as trust, intimacy, and communication. Those are subsets of areas stemming from love and respect.

Women want to be loved, and men want to be respected. It's that simple.

Here's an example of a coaching client experience that drives this point home.

> A married woman came to me for coaching. She states that she's not happy and feels no joy in her life. She has three children and has been married to her husband for ten years. We begin with her explaining some of the scenarios.
>
> *My husband works all of the time.*
>
> *We never spend time together because I'm busy with the kids and housework.*
>
> *He doesn't hang out with us on weekends.*

I explained to her what I stated previously: that men want to be respected. Here's what I challenged her to do:

1. When your husband arrives home from work, tell him how much you appreciate that he works so hard for your family and that you think he is a great provider.

2. Tell him, "It would mean a lot to me if we could have a date night once a week. I love spending time with you, and I miss just being a couple" (using "I" statements, eliminating defensive and blaming behavior).

3. Arrange an outing without the kids. A place or event to remind you of why you fell in love with one another. Be silly together and have fun!

4. Plan a family outing that he can participate in.

After three weeks of practicing this type of communication, my client said everything had changed! By changing her approach and showing gratitude, he made the adjustments needed to show her the love she wanted.

They went shopping together and dinner, dates, and laughter the whole time. Her husband was spending time with the kids and there was a shift back to fun and fulfillment.

Her husband now felt respected and in return expressed love and attention freely.

If we aren't feeling loved or that our needs are being met, as humans, we tend to grasp onto or seek someone from whom we can receive what we are looking for. This is how affairs start. A coworker or friend starts to listen and sympathize with our feelings and bam!

Suddenly we see this person as the other side of the fence. The grass is not greener over there; it's just temporarily being watered more than our side.

For men, it is very much feeling respected and needing physical affection (five love languages will verify that this is within the top three needs for men). Women need words of affirmation and quality time together.

Of course, there are some very toxic behaviors and characteristics that make working on a relationship nearly impossible. This is due to the fact that one person in the couple is the giver and one is the taker. Most partners with toxic qualities do not realize or acknowledge they are at fault. Many of them have personality disorders that can be changed through behavioral therapy but would never think they need it. Others are just stuck in a place and not ready to change no matter how detrimental it is to their spouse or relationship.

Addictions: The addict MUST want help for themselves; no ultimatum will ever work. They need to voluntarily seek the assistance and commit to a program. The injured spouse is usually codependent and enabling, fearing they will lose their mate.

Narcissism: This is a personality disorder and the affected must recognize the damage and/or hurt they cause. Unfortunately, it is difficult to get this person to recognize any fault since they are experts at gaslighting.

Here is the definition for gaslighting according to BING.com:

"Gaslighting is a form of psychological manipulation in which a person or a group covertly sows seeds of doubt in a targeted individual, making them question their own memory, perception, or judgment, often evoking in them cognitive dissonance and other changes such as low self-esteem. Using denial, misdirection, contradiction, and falsity, gaslighting involves attempts to destabilize the victim and delegitimize the victim's beliefs. Instances may range from the denial by an abuser that previous abusive incidents ever occurred to the staging of bizarre events by the abuser with the intention of disorientating the victim."

Abuse: This comes in many forms. From psychological to physical. The thing about abuse is that everyone seems to have a different definition and I believe it is why so many people remain in domestic violence relationships. For instance, if a spouse separates you from your family and friends and monitors your phone calls, but doesn't verbally abuse or physical hurt you, some say it is not abuse. It does not have to be the most extremely obvious form to be considered abuse. If anyone is taking away your freedom of being, whether financial, emotional, physical, or psychological—it is abuse. Do not be afraid to say something and get out of the situation.

I share with you my personal story of the abusive relationships I endured and yes, even allowed. By sharing with you, I solely intend to give you the understanding and insight of how it unfolds, the negative thoughts that are reinforced, and thankfully, how it can be overcome and viewed as an experience for which I can find gratitude. It took a long time to understand, overcome, and grow beyond these events, and I am grateful that I can look back at them with the knowledge of what they taught me, rather than just the regret of the time I spent within these unfulfilling relationships.

My story:

> I was eighteen years old and unsure of what the future held when I met my first husband. We were in high school when we met, fell in love, and believed it was destiny. Growing up in my home was difficult. Although I know my parents did the best they could, there were crucial emotional needs that weren't met.
>
> Sadly, my mother did not have a nurturing upbringing. She had a lot of expectations put on her that children shouldn't be burdened with. With her children, she tried the best she knew how based on the example she was given herself from her upbringing. I have come to understand she believed that providing the necessities (which she lacked as a child) was her way of showing love. I grew up feeling I lacked self-esteem. My mother wanted perfection and I just could not be perfect no matter how hard I tried.
>
> These feelings were magnified when I met my first husband. I felt loved, wholly, for the first time, and it sucked me in with every cell in my young body. I thought that love was all I would need to overcome any problems, and there were certainly problems with him and our relationship. The signs were there from the beginning, but I had no experience in my eighteen years to expect what was to come. He had a drug

addiction, which I agreed to help him overcome.

Yes, I believed I could fix him.

I soon moved in with him and became pregnant with my daughter Lacee. One day, we had an argument and he had me (three months' pregnant) up against the wall with his hand around my throat. I was in shock! The apologies came and promises that it would never happen again. Professing his undying love and need for me in his life solidified my resolve to help him.

He soon joined the military, without my knowing, and left me at home, alone, three months' pregnant. My parents had let me know that they didn't approve of my choice, especially the pregnancy, so I was distanced and shunned for quite a while.

After the birth of my daughter, which I endured completely terrified and alone in the delivery room, I called the Red Cross to let him know of her birth. He soon got stationed in Germany and for three months, I waited to join him with our newborn daughter.

Unfortunately, getting his wife and child by his side was not a priority.

He was drinking and partying until the day I called and said, "I'm coming to Germany. I bought a plane ticket." While living in Germany with no friends and family, we tried adjusting to this new family life. He would get stressed out, go drinking, come home and argue, and things would get violent. I remember one time being picked up and thrown across the room approximately six feet, landing on my ear on a chair.

My eardrum burst.

I called a girlfriend and went to stay with her. He called and began the apologizing routine. I explained that he needed help. We went to a mandated couples counselor provided by the military and it was completely ineffective.

After four years in Germany, we were transferred to a California base named Fort Ord, near Monterey. Although this was a better location, things just got more difficult. I was attending nursing school, working as a hostess at a restaurant, and taking care of two girls, now ages one and three.

The drinking and abuse continued, but the psychological thoughts from all of the preceding years kept me devoted to keeping the family together. I was expected to cook, clean, work, take care of the children, and even upkeep the yard. I was exhausted to say the least.

When my husband was finally discharged from the Army, we went back to Arizona, near our hometown, and tried to start a life. We rented a 600-square-foot townhome as he started automotive school and I worked as a nursing assistant on graveyard shift.

One night he failed to come home after work. He wouldn't call, or answer calls, and I was frantically calling hospitals and police stations. He rolled in drunk just before I had to go to work. I was so angry and let him know. This caused him to attack me; he pinned me down with his hand on my throat as I saw the darkness closing in. I remember thinking, *My girls can't find their mom dead on the floor. I have to do something.* I managed with superhuman strength to get my legs up to his shoulders to get him off. Those first breaths of air hurt my lungs and I realized I was so close to death. I shudder as I write this.

Did I leave then?

No, I did not.

I know you are thinking, *Why wouldn't you leave*, right? I now know I still had more lessons to learn from this experience. So, our so-called marriage continued on. The abuse continued, and he claimed he blacked out when he was doing these violent acts, which is possible. According to BING.com:

> *Alcohol-induced blackouts are caused by **excessive amounts of drinking, heavy drinking on an empty stomach, or binge drinking**, which causes your blood alcohol levels to rise very quickly. Although heavy drinking is often the cause of alcohol-induced blackouts, this is not always the case.*

We purchased a home in Scottsdale and things were getting better, or so I thought. He was closet drinking and one day I received a call from the credit card company questioning a charge I didn't make. I called and the credit card company had a recorded voice of John giving permission for the charge for a dating site he had been engaging on. I confronted him with this information and stated I would be divorcing him. He then admitted that he was an alcoholic and wanted to get help and needed me to support him. Very shortly thereafter, I found out I was pregnant with our third child, Noah.

How could I walk away now?

How am I going to do this alone?

I attended AA meetings and Al-Anon while pregnant, just praying it would work and we could have a "normal" life. Ten months after my son's birth, I found a letter in his truck with sexy pictures of a woman. I realized this had been occurring for quite some time. When I confronted him, he started to escalate the situation, and I knew where this led, so I just shut up. I will never forget, during this argument, my girls, six and eight, were at their little picnic table in the corner looking at me! It was truly my ah-ha moment, and I thought, *This is what they will think is normal and okay when they seek partners. I have to end this!*

I proceeded to file the divorce papers and begin the uphill climb of healing, surviving, and single parenthood.

During this time, I went full force into survival mode with children ages six, eight, and ten months old. Healing time? Hah! I didn't have time to pee, let alone heal. I didn't even know what that meant. I was definitely not self-aware, but focused on anything other than my struggles and making sure my kids were healthy and happy at that point in time.

About a year after the divorce, I met my second husband. He seemed like a knight in shining armor compared to what I had just gone through for the last eleven years. Although a good husband, he was not able to be an understanding and patient stepparent. I had always made sure to put my children first. This never wavered, so my own wants would have to take a backseat.

We divorced after four years as I realized I was never truly in love with him. It just felt safe, was a good friendship, and I enjoyed an abuse-free relationship. I was not healed. One year later I met someone. This person was at the same level of abuse psychologically as my first husband was physically. A closet drinker, unemployed, and a sociopath, he stole my bank card every chance he could, gambled, and pathologically lied as easily as most of us breathe. He was charismatic and played a part so well that everyone liked him.

I was gaslighted on the regular to believe I was crazy and that he wasn't abusing me or taking advantage of me. He was obsessed with me and wouldn't let me leave the house except to work. He would call or text every fifteen minutes. My health suffered as I was diagnosed with cervical cancer, skin cancer, rheumatoid arthritis, and began walking with a cane.

I finally realized how dysfunctional this relationship was. I was able to remove him from my home, although he stalked and harassed me for years. I took my power back and didn't give him energy I could put into starting to love myself.

After a year dating another man, who also was narcissistic, I decided to stop the madness.

I knew the healing had to happen. I had to understand why I experienced these cycles of the same type of man again and again. Why was I allowing and attracting this over and over? I dug deep down and had to face my shortcomings, my fears, my insecurities, and what part I played in the cyclic behavior I kept performing.

I began learning self-care and how to forgive myself. The biggest belief I finally instilled in myself was that "I am worthy, and I have choices." I immersed myself in hiking, reading, and enjoying life, alone. I discontinued all medication and became healthy again. I learned to enjoy my own company. I started helping others and speaking my truth and learning what boundaries are.

I finally knew that I was whole. That I could validate and love who I am. That I was amazing, and I was here on this planet for greatness. I was content with my life and excited about the future for the first time in over a decade!

After two years of growing and healing, I decided to register on a dating site, where I received an email from a nice gentleman. After four months of conversation, I finally agreed to meet him for dinner. We spent six hours together on our first date, which I tried to sabotage unsuccessfully, thank goodness, because this was the man who would finally be the yin to my yang, who I now know is my twin flame (one soul split into two until reunited), my now husband, Dennis.

I finally understand why the healing is so important. I don't have a partner who must fix me or vice versa. I have a partner who I am free to be myself with. I am understood and loved unconditionally now because...I first loved who I am.

That was my journey. I also have a child who made similar choices and had similar experiences. As a parent, it was gut-wrenching to watch and feel completely helpless to seeing the pain. Even though I had firsthand knowledge that I needed to go through it, saving my child became my priority. For years, I would enable her by trying to remove her from dire situations with harmful men and choices, only to see her go back and ask for the trials again and again.

It was when I had to let go and let her fully feel the pain that she would then grow.

> **Lacee's Story:** Being raised in a home with divorced parents is never easy. Having a father who, at most, would see them every other weekend, if he decided to show up, probably took a bigger toll on my daughter than I would have expected. Lacee met her first husband at sixteen years old. After dating for a few months, Lacee became pregnant at seventeen with her son. Similar to my first husband, Lacee's husband liked to party, and the two of them started off with all odds against them. She really loved him and wanted it to work, but at that age, they really weren't equipped with the maturity to understand the work needed.
>
> They did eventually marry and had two more children (beautiful baby girls), but there were not many changes to his behavior. After years of struggle, he did not keep a steady job and became more controlling and had addictions to drugs and alcohol. Eventually, it fell apart after some domestic violence issues and financial hardship, and she divorced him.
>
> She had not grown, nor did she value herself, and shortly after her divorce, she met a man who would become her second husband. He was also abusive and

controlling, but in a much different way, so initially, she believed he was different. He was much more controlling and physically abusive. It eventually climaxed to him breaking her arm, and she had to have surgery that installed a plate and screws. Her arm will never be the same, and the daily pain reminds her of how she has been able to recover and never allow that type of behavior again. Here is how she worked through the traumatic experience and discovered what steps she needed to take to heal and even learn from this:

Here is an interview in her words:

1. **What was your most painful or impactful moment**? I was always that girl who said she would never be in a domestic violence relationship, and then I realized I was in one.

2. **How did it begin?** I was just so broken after going through a difficult and tumultuous divorce; he came in and I saw him as someone who would save me, my knight in shining armor, you could say.

3. **What red flags do you believe you missed or overlooked?** I ignored his past. I made excuses for all the bad things that he said happened to him or that he did to exes or family.

4. **What was your ah-ha moment?** There really wasn't one. It was a progression over the year that he kept me isolated with no communication from my family and pulled me away from my kids. I started to grow and get stronger or at least start to realize it wasn't going to change no matter how hard I tried.

5. **Were there any episodes of physical abuse and violence?** Many. The ones that stand out are the time he abandoned me in Santa Cruz (two hours from our home) with no phone, car, or money. I was alone, scared, and stranded. He drove himself all the way home drunk in my car. And then when he broke my arm. A violent break, where he threw me on the bed, and I heard it crack. All the while driving me to the emergency room, he was intimidating and threatening me not to report him. I still protected him until one day I left to visit my family in another state and never came back.

6. **What would you say to your daughters if they were in that situation?** There's not a lot you can say; they would have to go through it. I would (and do) just instill in them to know their worth and not fall for anyone's manipulation of them.

7. **What will you do differently when you heal and start dating again?** I will not overlook red flags. I will question everything. I know what I am worth, and I will not seek a relationship but let it come to me.

8. **What advice would you give someone about healing from a traumatic or unhealthy relationship?** That it takes time. Do not feel shame about your story, do things alone and learn to love yourself, and never rely on someone else for your happiness!

Chapter 7

CONTENTMENT IS
UNDERRATED

When I say contentment, what is the first thing that pops into your mind?

Here's the definition:

contentment

[kənˈtentmənt]

NOUN

1. a state of happiness and satisfaction.

In this world of overstimulation and constant hustle, "contentment" would equal or be viewed as boring or complacency.

Complacency is defined as a feeling of smug or uncritical satisfaction with oneself or one's achievements. I actually don't think that's a bad thing either.

So why have we been programmed to think either of these represents an unfulfilled or uneventful life? When I think about words that people would use to describe an exciting or satisfying life, it would be more like hustle, stimulating, adventurous, risk-taking, embellished, exhilarating. Although yes, these are good, they are momentary actions or feelings, not long-term sustainable. From this come the words and phrases to describe the mental state and increasing mental illness in this country such as burnout, stress, overwhelmed, stuck, over it, and exhausted.

As I am sitting in my kitchen in the breakfast nook, I have three large windows next to me. Outside, it is sunny and cool on a beautiful day in February. My pups Jade and Brodie are on the couches sleeping and Callie is on the floor by my feet. That is contentment. They could be doing ANYTHING else on this glorious afternoon. But right now, they feel like resting. When they spontaneously jump up and bark at the mail carrier or another dog being walked by its owner, they are still in a place of contentment because they are consistently doing what feels most enjoyable to them.

They don't mind staying home when I must run an errand or even go on a vacation.

They don't need new furniture or even new toys every day.

They don't need to be entertained, or at least not much more than a walk or a game of fetch. They are so happy with their people and their environment. As long as they are loved and cared for and their needs are met, they are joyful and satisfied.

Do you remember observing your parents or grandparents' relationships when you were younger? Did it seem like they were so boring and disengaged? I remember watching my parents' marriage and thinking, *No way, I won't have a marriage like that.* My parents have now been married for almost fifty-five years! Guess what? They are content and in spite of, or because of, the years with difficulty and inevitable growth, it worked for them.

We will only feel a discord in our interconnections if the partner is not a good fit or match for us. The relationship will inevitably fail, or we will sustain in silent unalignment and un-fulfillment. It is okay to walk or run from any relationship that no longer serves you. It's okay to grow apart and accept it. It's okay to say, "We tried for many years and gave it our best." It's okay to say, "I lived and learned, and I am ready for my next phase of expansion." There's a saying in social work with couples: "You didn't fail; the relationship failed." I don't exactly agree with that and I would say, "We succeeded in growing, and the relationship helped us do that."

As I write this, we are currently facing a pandemic virus, COVID-19. Everyone is quarantined and requested to stay at home. Restaurants, gyms, stores, and schools have all closed. As I look at social media, I notice there are predominantly two types of people.

I am seeing those who are reporting all of the negative and scary news, and those who are creating funny memes and inspirational quotes.

Most others fall in between.

What I have noticed is that those people who I know personally and are in a happy state of mind are taking everything in stride while we wait for news of what's to come. Those are content people. Although I can get pretty stir crazy, I am very happy staying home, writing this book, planting a garden, and playing with the furry babies.

After finally meeting my husband, Dennis, and settling into what is now our routine, I now understand how wonderful contentment is. It is the comfort of knowing what to expect from a partner, knowing I am loved no matter what life or situations bring, knowing I can count on him in so many ways.

I've always heard that "marriage is work." And to be honest, every relationship prior to my marriage WAS work—backbreaking, emotionally draining work—because it wasn't what I have now. The flow of marriage depends on how the couple chooses to engage in it. Work indicates that our life is obligatory and filled with tasks we don't want to do. That is not how it should be.

Dennis and I find ways to make each other happy every... single...day. It's a genuine desire to do this. We don't keep score; we don't do it for self-gratification or to seek validation. We love unconditionally and put the other person's happiness as a priority. Even in moments of disagreement, I don't feel marriage is work. It's so meaningful to find ways to be in a peaceful place of contentment.

My apologies, contentment and complacency. My perception of you was all wrong.

Chapter 8

THAT IS SO WEIRD

Now that you've found your person or you've been in a relationship for a while or married for many years, how do you keep the bond and connection strong?

I will address many areas and ideas to help you along, in no particular order. You will find the ones that pertain to your coupling situation.

Without fail, every time I use the restroom, one of the furry babies thinks they need to join me. They must believe that I will be so lonely for the two whole minutes I've secluded myself away from my little creatures, and that I will be doomed if they don't keep me company. Our downstairs guest bathroom has a doggy door next to the commode. This is so the pups (and kitty) can come and go outside to the backyard. Many a guest has been quite surprised by the entrance of one or more of the furry babies while relieving themselves. Jade feels she needs to stand with her front paws on my knees and get belly rubs when the occasion arises. When I shower, my gray Bengal kitty, Grayson, needs to sit on the side of the tub and apparently protect me from whatever forces are outside of the shower curtain, all while getting his tail soaked sitting at his post.

They don't understand nor really care about giving me my personal space. Do you remember when you were first dating someone, and you would sit on the couch and snuggle? Then, as your comfort level increased, one person was in the bedroom and the other on the couch. This transition is okay. We need to give one another space to do our own thing. If your "thing" as a couple is to be together every waking minute, then that is your prerogative. Most of us need that alone time—time to get away and breathe or think.

In many relationships, we can suffocate one another by consistently needing attention. The attention we seek is validation. Validation is a human need; however, it does grow weary when you seek ALL of your validation from your partner. It is very healthy to seek validation in other ways. Have outside interests, friends, and groups in addition to the relationship. This gives you more to talk about with one another and gives you time to recharge and decompress from the day.

Eventually, a relationship without giving space will not make it. I don't even know where my husband is most of the time in the house and I usually have to text him from the other room if I need anything. I don't ask permission for outings with my girlfriends or to go for a hike. I let him know and write it on the calendar. I let him know that I am going out, and of course to take care of the animals while I am away. I encourage his alone time as well. I practically push him out the door to go golfing or to the gym. We are a "you do you" kind of couple.

*"We are all a little weird and life is a little weird, and when we find someone whose **weirdness** is compatible with ours, we join up with them and fall in mutual **weirdness** and call it **love**."*
—Dr. Seuss

About six months ago, a girlfriend of mine met with someone she knew from high school. They reunited and began building a relationship. One day, I went to her house and I was greeted by the new boyfriend. He was wearing something I thought was peculiar for a grown man. It was like a grown-up onesie, similar to the pajamas with the snaps in the nether regions we would put on our children as newborn babies. I did a double-take and said, "I'm so glad you are comfortable with your manhood."

Hey, who am I to judge? The takeaway from that for me was that we all have these idiosyncrasies that others may find weird. And others may find them adorable.

Grayson, my kitty, will be sleeping on the floor, and out of nowhere, Jade, my chihuahua, will run and jump on his back. Callie, the border collie, drops her ball down the stairs over and over and over...thump, thump, thump, runs down to fetch it, then runs back up and does it again. Brodie, our Aussie, is getting older and has hip dysplasia. He wakes me up every morning around 2:00 to turn on the hall light by the stairs just to cheer him on and let him know he can get up the stairs. He doesn't need me to assist him. I just stand at the top and say, "Come on, you can do it, good boy!"

My husband, Dennis, loves Corgi breed dogs. He's never had one, and we don't have one now. However, every...single...day...he sends a picture or video or GIF with a Corgi. Like clockwork. And I respond with a coordinating emoji. We just get each other.

It's pretty endearing if you choose to look with love and not judgment.

Remember the weird things our parents did? Do you ever "people watch" and wonder how someone's spouse or partner handles their oddities? See an odd couple and smile at the fact that there is a yin for everyone's yang? What are your own quirks? Do you think you do something that others would find weird? Sometimes it is hard to look at ourselves and identify anything we do as weird because, well, it's just us and what we've always done. I think we are all so unique and special, and that's what makes it fun and hilarious to live in this world, coexisting and observing one another.

Chapter 9

THAT IS NOT FUNNY

I was talking on the phone with a man I had just met as I was a guest on a podcast he produces. He told me that when he talks to women he's interested in, they don't get his humor, yet everyone is looking for someone with a sense of humor. I thought about that and he's right. Then I told him that humor is subjective, not objective. He likes the sort of old-school humor of Monty Python and it would take a specific person to like that style of humor.

Have you ever told a joke and got crickets from your audience? That's because the perception of humor is also part of the experiences we've learned. I find that I have similar humor taste to what my father likes. Sort of a sarcastic and witty humor. Or physical humor like Jim Carrey in *Pet Detective*. As I think about my children, I realize they all have my same sense of humor. Their preference for certain types of humor is part of their programming because laughter releases endorphins and makes us feel euphoric. If my children made me laugh, they witnessed a sense of happiness and fun that they enjoyed and wanted to continue. It became a part of their habits that created joy in their life.

The tricky part about humor is that it is like the other vibrations and we strive to meet someone at the same level.

My husband and I differ on our enjoyment of comedic entertainment. He likes cartoons such as *South Park* or *Rick and Morty*. I don't get this kind of humor. It doesn't resonate with me. I like watching *The Connors* because it's pretty similar to the way my family spoke to one another. He doesn't find this funny. However, we love to watch certain shows that we both find funny. We meet in the middle and watch together.

In researching, I didn't realize there was such a vast array of types of comedy and humor. As different as we all are as people, it would make sense that this is like any other specific trait we look for in our partners.

Here are some different types of comedy: Which ones do you enjoy? Be sure to attract someone who enjoys similar humor. The couple that plays together stays together.

> **Slapstick Comedy** - The humor in slapstick derives from its exaggerated physical gesturing, movements, and situations.
>
> **Deadpan** - Deadpan is exactly what it sounds like: delivering jokes without any noticeable change in emotion. A comic from the 1990s named Steven Wright was one of the best deadpan comics I can recall.
>
> **Self-Deprecating** - These are things that most common people can relate to, and so it becomes a tension reliever to laugh at our own problems encompassed by another.

Potty Humor - A type of humor that focuses on making the audience cringe. It's often in poor taste, vulgar, and "crosses the line" for the sake of making people laugh.

Topical Humor - It's easy and accessible humor that makes fun of current events.

Satire - Satire is not just the art of mocking something; it's about using irony, sarcasm, and caricature to highlight the real-life vices and flaws about the thing you're satirizing, while still making relevant social commentary about that thing.

Parody - Parody is about mocking something through imitation. This can be done out of a distaste for the thing being parodied, or as a playful tribute.

Dark Comedy - Dark comedy, also called black comedy or gallows humor, is a type of humor that focuses on serious, dark, and often morbid subject matter.

Surreal Comedy - Surreal comedy is about defying logic and using nonsensical situations and non-sequiturs to get a laugh out of people. It's easy to equate it to slapstick, as the two can sometimes overlap, but surreal comedy leans much more toward the bizarre. Many TikTok videos use surreal comedy.

The one thing we do all agree on in my household are the silly antics of the furry babies. When you watch your pets, you realize how funny they can be, not to mention that they are not self-conscious about their crazy behavior. They just don't care what anyone thinks, and that's what we can take away from this chapter.

I've realized some canine breeds and feline breeds are funnier than others. If you watch TikTok videos, there's a plethora of French bulldogs, chihuahuas, and dachshunds that are quite mischievous. I favor border collies since both of my adult daughters own one and I have witnessed their abundance of personality. Callie, my daughter's border collie, keeps us continuously entertained. We call her "derpy" because she's so carefree and goofy. She places bones, toys, and balls in our swimming pool to see if they float. She will get onto the steps and try to paddle them back to her. She is an endless provider of the endorphins released in our brains when watching her each day.

The lesson is to free yourself and enjoy the humorous aspects of the world and appreciate the laughter in and around you.

Chapter 10

NOT YOUR CUP OF TEA

One of the biggest components within a relationship is sex. However, there is a difference between sex and sex-u-al-it-y...

As in the previous chapters, I discuss how important it is to stick to a list of things you desire; to maintain your "bar." To stay true to yourself and find the match and compatible partner you want. This chapter will also apply to my long-timers and committed couples.

In this forward-thinking day and age, it is a wonder why the talk of sex still makes the most liberal of us blush or cringe. It is rare to find an individual who can speak freely about sex and sexuality.

I'm not going to compare our human sexuality to that of the furry babies. I have learned that sex is one of the fundamental differences between us and the animal kingdom. For the most part, animals engage in intercourse solely for reproduction and continuation of their species. I know that there are some exceptions, but in general, humans have sex for pleasure

AND procreation. However, while researching for this chapter I found some (astonishing) information. Humans are not the only ones who derive pleasure from the physical act. Oral sex is well documented in mammals as diverse as **rats, fruit bats, horses, goats, dolphins, most primates, cheetahs, lions, hyenas, sheep, and cattle**. How a scientist discovered some of these aspects would be a mystery as far as I'm concerned, and honestly I'm grateful that my career path did not include this type of research.

I've noticed there are definitive lines of belief drawn when it comes to this subject. Most comes from our childhood programming and how liberal or conservative our households were about communicating about the content. Religion is also a large factor in our openness about sex and sexuality. Additionally, there are also perspectives created from personal experience.

For example, if you had a conservative upbringing, you may have carried the belief that sex is not to be spoken of outside of the bedroom. Religious training may include warnings and prohibitions regarding sex before marriage and masturbation. If you perhaps had an unhealthy relationship with someone who used sex as a tool or made a derogatory statement about your physical appearance or sexual performance, or convinced you that you were only valued if you "gave it up," this would also skew your view of healthy sexual encounters.

Let's go further and explore opinions regarding the LGBTQ (lesbian, gay, bisexual, transgender, and queer) community. I have become a part of a business community that supports the LGBTQ community with equal opportunity and no discrimination in professional environments. Those who have been discriminated and judged the most, I find, are the most willing to make changes and accept that which they cannot change—the outside opinions of others.

We tend to listen to the views of others on this subject. This is like anything else that carries strong emotional feelings whether it be race, religion, or politics. I believe everyone is entitled to their beliefs as long as they are not being forced on anyone else and we don't judge others for their choices and beliefs.

A recent and evolving description of a sexual preference is pansexual or fluid. This is having an attraction to someone regardless of gender. In other words, being attracted to the soul or being of someone. I feel this is an elevated and enlightened way to view others.

Regardless of sexual attraction, shouldn't we all be attracted to the core and vibration of others in the first place? Shouldn't the genuineness and kindness of someone matter most? Have you ever met someone and instantly hit it off or it feels like you have known them for a long time? Tune yourself into recognizing these feelings as you sort through the relationship and friendship arenas.

That is a good spot to leave sexual equality and dig in to how to have a healthy sexual relationship with your chosen one.

What's your fancy?

Finding a sexually compatible partner is a critical aspect of a relationship. The most vital piece of this is to be brave and open to communicating your needs. Accept that you are free to choose and express who you are. This is important whether you are a highly sexual being with specific needs or you have low sexual energy so that sex is not high on your priority list for a relationship.

No matter where you fall on this spectrum of sexuality and sexual needs, do not allow anyone to shame you or coerce you into anything that you are not comfortable with. Based on your belief system, just be open about discussing these needs when entering into a potentially committed union, or even a short-term relationship. Also, your sexual agency (the ability to say yes or no to sex) is yours and yours alone, and can be given and withdrawn at any time.

On a more serious note, of course this is easy to say and harder in real life. Our sexual needs and experiences vary throughout our life, and each person's experience is different. There are many people who have had earlier sexual experiences that were negative. This can create a fundamental issue with sex and one that may be difficult to overcome. Negative sexual experiences can happen to anyone at any age. The impact can influence a person's sexual viewpoint, drive, and openness until they can overcome or deal with the emotions associated with these experiences.

While this book is not a guide for sex and sex-related issues, it is something that needs to be included within most relationships. If you are the victim of negative sexual experiences, I certainly recommend that you seek help from a qualified professional. It's helpful to seek out someone who can also break down any triggers from past sexual trauma, such as abuse, rape, or molestation. To have a fulfilling relationship, a person needs to work to get past any blockage related to intimacy.

Let's keep the spark alive...

We need to address the difference in sexual drive between men and women. As noted previously, there is no one measure that would accurately describe every woman and every man. However, there are some interesting statistics and facts when you look into the subject:

> "Men want sex more often than women at the start of a relationship, in the middle of it, and after many years of it," Roy Baumeister, PhD Psychology, concludes after reviewing several surveys of men and women (*www.web-md.com*). This isn't just true of heterosexuals, he says; gay men also have sex more often than lesbians at all stages of the relationship. Men also say they want more sex partners in their lifetime and are more interested in casual sex.
>
> Women were more likely than men to show inconsistency between their expressed values about sexual activities such as premarital sex and their actual behavior.
>
> - Women's attitudes toward (and willingness to perform) various sexual practices are more likely than men's to change over time.
>
> - Women who regularly attend church are less likely to have permissive attitudes about sex. Men do not show this connection between church attendance and sex attitudes.
>
> - Women are more influenced by the attitudes of their peer group in their decisions about sex.

The importance of a good intimate relationship is indicated by infidelity by people in committed relationships. The key reason men commit infidelity in relationships is because the physical needs and affection are not being met. I have performed an informal survey of the men I have encountered and found that for 90 percent of them, their number one love language is physical affection. Not that surprising, right? It's more than just the sex; it's a scientific theory that goes back to the beginning of Neanderthal men needing to "spread their seed" or reproduce for species continuation. Let's credit today's male gender with more than that need and add to it that ego and the need for respect are closer to truth.

When we enter a committed relationship, the ingredients should include mental, emotional, spiritual, and physical connection for complete fulfillment. If you are giving and getting these, then you proceed with the agreement. In essence, you have created a "contract" that these will continue to be given. As time goes by and you get comfortable with a partner, unfortunately, complacency rears its ugly head. The partners can get lazy or feel "I've already got them, so I don't have to put in as much effort as I did at the beginning." This is what causes the lapse in physical connection in most cases.

Let's give a visual analogy. When you move into a new home, it looks and smells new and exciting. As time goes on, repairs and maintenance must continuously be performed or the house will crumble. A relationship is the same in that we must continue to pay attention to detail and maintain it.

If you feel things are getting stagnant or mundane, it's up to you to be creative and find ways to keep the spark of sexual activity and connectivity alive. Both partners must be willing to contribute and be open to the needs of the other. If a partner approaches with new and different suggestions regarding their needs (sexual or not), be sure to appreciate the honest communication they are giving. Know that it takes bravery to be open about your sexual needs, especially when those needs may be different than what has been expressed or experienced in the past. And know that this discussion is a very healthy part of a positive relationship.

Many couples find that exploring new things such as open relationships, positions, and sex accessories adds adventure and excitement. If you are in a meaningful and healthy relationship, you can have an open mind to any and all things your partner suggests and be honest if it's not something you are comfortable with.

The bottom line is that anything that brings satisfaction to your partner and yourself is your business. Remove any shame, embarrassment, and childhood or religious programming and stigmas you may have picked up along your journey and see how exciting your intimacy and physical fulfillment can be!

Chapter 11

THE FINAL ROSE

The most recent season of a popular show on television has just finished as I write this book. It involved someone single attempting to "date" twenty-five potential partners and hoping to get engaged at the end. Beyond the entertainment of the show, I really want to review the interesting psychology of what ensued.

When the young man goes through the process, he tends to be attracted to the more outspoken, and yes, dramatic women. When you see the hometown date with his family, you can see that he has a mother who is a very strong, opinionated, and emotional woman (she displays this by crying and passionately explaining what she wants for her son). Is it any wonder he is attracted to the same type of woman? No, it is not a cliché that we choose partners similar to our parents. This is the programming and observation that infiltrate our subconscious minds as we grow in childhood.

Fast-forward to the end of the show, where our bachelor is in love with the two final women. He actually states that he is in love with two women! One of the women realizes that they have different morals and lifestyles and chooses to leave (she is quite aligned it would seem). Our bachelor is heartbroken, but recovers in two days, or at least enough to decide to propose to the remaining woman, whom his family is very approving of. (So much for true love!) Yet, he discovers within a month afterward that he's just not feeling that strongly about her. He, then, is reunited with the first woman, who now decides she would like to give a relationship a chance with him.

First, this roller coaster is exactly why we are compelled to watch. And know that I am in no way criticizing or judging this storyline, as these are real people with real feelings experiencing a pretty common scenario in an unconventional way.

Second, for me, watching this show unfold was relationships and dating 101. Why is it that we do the behavior that makes choosing so difficult? This man assumably had not healed from previous rejection (he was the runner-up from last season) and was "hoping" to figure it out along the way. He stated, "I'm following my heart," but he should have followed his Spirit and healed to know his worth, and the clarity would have been there, instead of the emotional roller coaster he experienced. This is what most of us do. Once you're healed and whole with your past and you know clearly what your "bar" is, the choosing becomes much easier.

Many of us have experienced the tug-of-war between two people we were dating. Sometimes our conflicted emotions are over two people who are equally attractive and of similar personalities. Sometimes one is the safe bet and the other stirs our "bad boy/girl" desires. Often, usually in our younger years, we gravitate toward the person who seems to be a challenge. It is almost as though we are determined to "win" this person over and make them love us. Hah! The energy that goes into this endeavor is generally wasted. Youth (and the infinite energy of youth) is wasted on the young I have heard, and this is something that I did when I was a young dater.

When strong feelings or love for someone are not shared or reciprocated, it can be a painful process.

Even when you meet someone and they initially share feelings of attraction or love, circumstances and events can change our opinion of another, and our relationship is lost (or dies) with this change. This leads to breakups and rejection.

In my opinion, and validated by many psychologists, the two most important human needs are acceptance and validation. It is no wonder that breakups and rejection are the most painful experiences we can encounter. It goes straight to the core of our human need and deprives us of joy and comfort. It gets engrained and programmed into our psyche and subconscious as a memory that we don't want to relive.

That being said, being able to recover and heal from the experience can be the hardest thing anyone can go through. It makes letting go of the past extremely difficult since it is a traumatic time in life for most people. It is a negative hit to our self-image, identity, self-esteem, and perspective of ourselves. It can also trigger feelings of inadequacy we may have had programmed from childhood from critical or negative relatives. It just hurts our hearts, minds, and spirits to the core.

So then, how do any of us recover from this?

There is no easy way to get through any painful ordeal. However, here are some positive methods of recovery.

1. **Breathe, breathe, breathe:** As a standard operating procedure for my life coaching practice, I would

always suggest meditation. There are many varieties and levels. Whether you're starting out the day or ending the day, or anytime you are feeling emotionally overwhelmed, meditation will bring you back to feeling more in control and even trusting that the process is working. The attracting of the experiences you face will give you a sense of accomplishment and learning.

There are certain sound vibrations for different needs. For example, 432 hertz (hz) and 528 hz are healing frequencies, while 396 hz helps let go of anxiety, worries, and fears. Imagery meditation is also a great way to clear your mind.

When my daughter Lacee finally left an abusive marriage and moved back home, I would ask her to meditate. One session, we chose an imagery meditation where we were guided to carry a long rope with an anchor. The anchor was our past pain and current fears and anxiety. We were on a beach and guided to find a pair of shiny scissors and cut the rope. We were then directed to meet our future selves on the beach, where they would hug us and thank us. It was a very healing meditation and we still think about it when we have any struggle or conflict. It helps us to realize that our future selves will be stronger and healed based on the understanding and perseverance of how we handle our today.

2. **Sit with your friend, Mr. Feelings:** I once had a session with a life coach at the beginning of my own journey. At the time, I was feeling quite a bit of guilt over my eldest daughter's situation in life that was less than

ideal. I felt I had caused certain programming that led her to the decisions and choices she was making. This life coach told me that it was okay to sit with my feelings of guilt, not to suppress or ignore them, but invite them in for coffee, but then ask them to leave.

I couldn't let them stay for a sleepover or take a vacation with them.

In other words, go ahead and process the emotions, soothe yourself in knowing that your hurt is valid, but then set a time limit and say, "Okay, now we move forward." It's a spin on doing release work. It also helps ease shame by allowing yourself to own your actions and choices.

3. **Get out there!** Go do something physical! Join a yoga group, go hiking, join a boxing gym, walk a labyrinth. You need a release. While doing a physical activity, you will produce endorphins that will lift your energy and your mood. It will also boost your self-esteem and help you realize that you are strong and whole without a partner. Joining with others who share your interests also opens the door to new friendships, which leads to finding connections and opportunities to occupy your time and your mind.

4. **Talk to me, baby**! It will be so crucial in your healing to speak positively to yourself. Try not to beat yourself up or instill any thoughts and beliefs that you aren't enough. Reframing is so important at this time. When you are thinking self-deprecating thoughts, turn those around into positives.

Here are a few examples:

"I'll never find love"—I'm so worthy, my person is very rare, and it will take a little more time for us to find one another. I'm getting closer every day.

"I always screw relationships up. What is wrong with me?"—I know what I want and what I do not want. My new choices are mine. I am a great catch and I love unconditionally.

"I'm so exhausted and emotionally drained"—I will take care of me as priority for today. I will find things that make me feel good and enjoy each day. I will enjoy my own company and go with the flow.

5. **Is it counterproductive?** This may sound like an unconventional way, but I found that it works well for me to write or discuss my relationship issues and failures. I have either journaled or reminded myself of the things that hadn't worked in a relationship that I began healing from. It's not that I wanted to rehash and relive the negative feelings or experience, but I remembered the instances when the ex-boyfriend or ex-husband left. By remembering what I *didn't* want, I was reinforcing what I *do* want in moving forward to my next relationship. It also helped me get a better perspective and even take accountability for my behavior in those past relationships for more self-awareness.

6. **Mirror, Mirror:** I really believe the most impactful and harmful act we do as humans is compare ourselves to others. Rejection can be so difficult in today's world because of the overwhelming exposure to watching

what others are doing. It instills in us the belief that we are not "keeping up with the..." or that we should be further along in career, family, relationship, kids, financial goals, etc.

During a breakup, it would be a great time to unplug from social media. Focus only on nurturing relationships with friends and family who really love and appreciate you. Be mindful about sifting through what others say. For instance, if a friend really liked your ex, they may try to convince you that the ex-partner wasn't so bad and deserves a second chance.

Try not to repeatedly speak about the relationship, as this just brings more negative energy and slows down the healing process. When we separate from someone and others want to know the details, we can just say, "It just didn't work out; we aren't a good fit for one another." You don't owe anyone an in-depth explanation of every incident and situation that caused your breakup. The sooner you accept the truth and understanding about a relationship, the sooner you can heal and look to the future that you desire.

This may sound like the exact opposite of the method described in #5, and it is! These techniques are not one-size-fits-all; rather they are methods for you to consider and use on your relationship journey.

7. **Self-Soothe:** I am a firm believer in rewarding ourselves for our accomplishments. When you've been through a difficult time, it's especially important to be kind to yourself. Go get a nice relaxing massage. Go

buy a new outfit, get a new haircut, eat your favorite ice cream, or take a solo trip to your dream destination. Doing anything that makes you feel better and affirms that you deserve happiness is going to help in the healing process. It also builds self-confidence and confirms that singlehood can be fun and empowering. It shows you that you alone can do anything.

8. **Set those goals:** Goal setting for the future, creating a vision board, and performing a daily affirmation are ways to stay focused on your goals. One of the other things that I encourage my clients to do is intention setting.

Every morning before you get out of bed, close your eyes and speak what you want your day to look like. Saying your intentions out loud is critical. This is creating the possibilities and a way of feeling more in control. Instead of waiting to see what the day brings, say this: "Today will be a great day. I will learn new things, meet new people, bring more opportunities. I will stay in alignment and know that I have the power over my life."

To further this boost of self-encouragement, I ask my clients to create a mantra, such as "I am enough," or have a power song like the Rocky theme song, "Eye of the Tiger."

Music is so healing and important within our lives.

My father is a musician. He has played all kinds of instruments from guitar to keyboard and was in a Beatles cover band in Chicago in his younger days. He also is a member of a songwriter's group. One day we were having one of our discussions about life, which occurs every time we are together. He was talking about how important lyrics are. That they have a "hook." If you think about your favorite song, you will notice there is an impactful chorus or phrase that resonates with you. I always felt that listening to music was like a therapy with the realization that someone else went through the same circumstances that I did.

When I have a big meeting or opportunity to attend, I will play "Unstoppable" by Sia. While going through my divorce, I would listen to "You Oughta Know" by Alanis Morissette. It was a song that I could sing at the top of my lungs and release some of the anger and betrayal I had experienced. I used to call it my "crazy hate music."

What's your power song?

What's a good mantra that keeps you going forward?

I love to tell myself, "Everything always works out for me." It reaffirms and reframes my thoughts when I'm in the middle of something difficult. I remind myself of all the times I have made it through and come out better on the other side. It diminishes my frustration in the present moment by allowing me to be clearer about why I am having to participate in the current obstacle.

9. **Break the habit:** A pertinent fact in recovering from a painful breakup is that we have made this partner a "habit." They became a part of our daily routine. We'll

miss the stability of the person, so to speak. We'll check our phones, our email, our messages, and realize the "loss" of the habit. If they liked a particular thing, we get melancholy just seeing it, or smelling it, or tasting it. All of these reasons enforce the need to change the habit.

Change the routine.

If you sat and had coffee each morning with the ex, go to the gym or take a walk instead. If they enjoyed rock music, change the station and listen to country music. You create new habits out of creating the new desire for different thoughts. Smile at the past but laugh with the future.

Newness is intriguing and exciting.

Remember when you tried a food that you now love for the first time? You did it—you went out on a scary limb and did something you had not done before. Overcoming the habit of a previous affair of the heart is all about facing the unknown without the person. You must do the work though. Feel the feels, think the thoughts, and then say, "I'm ready to move forward."

It is interesting to watch the furry babies when they are faced with a challenge. They will try to get the ball out from under the couch by walking around it, trying to use their paw, barking at it, or digging at the floor. Obviously, most of these techniques don't work, but the strength of willpower and persistence is admirable. They don't give up and neither should you!

Overcoming the loss associated with a relationship will take time. It may take more than one of the techniques I described or one that you think of for yourself. The keys are patience, kindness with yourself and your feelings, and recognition of your growth through the process.

Chapter 12

THE LINE IN THE SAND

*E*very afternoon, I give each furry friend a snack. Sometimes they each get a chewy bone, which is the favorite treat, or a bacon strip treat. I hand one to each baby, and they go off to a separate place in the yard to enjoy their treasure. Jade usually gobbles hers up quickly. Brodie is a more complacent pup when it comes to personal space; however, when it's time for their treat, if either dog comes near him, it's game on. He shows his teeth and makes it clear to the others to stay away.

Since Jade is small in stature but large in personality, when we are at the dog park and specific dogs come up to her, she stands her ground, scrunches her nose, curls her lip, and gives a little snap to let them know they are not welcome.

These are the ways that my dogs enforce their personal boundaries.

According to www.recoveryeducationnetwork.org, a boundary is:

Emotional and physical space between you and another person. Demarcation of where you end and another begins, and where you begin and another ends. Limit or line over which you will not allow anyone to cross because of the negative impact of its being.

Boundaries in all relationships are vital to our feeling safe and respected. Whether it's interfamilial, friendship, business, or romantic relationships, boundaries must be respected by both parties. There are different categories of boundaries: physical, psychological, emotional, and spiritual.

Physical boundaries are exactly as they sound, setting personal space and physical contact limitations of comfort level.

Here is an example of how the physical boundary can be violated:

According to Chester McNaughton (a registered professional counselor who specializes in boundaries, anger management, and dysfunctional relationships in Edmonton, Alberta, Canada), boundary violations typically fall into three categories: aggressive, passive-aggressive, or accidental.

Aggressive violations include shoving and hitting; damaging property; exerting control over someone's time or money; making threats; taunting and hurling insults.

Passive-aggressive behavior in relationships results in psychological, emotional, and spiritual boundaries being violated and are generally one person in the relationship taking control of someone else's beliefs, preferences, and feelings. Passive-aggressive behavior can be more insidious, since it generally happens over time, but is just as effective as aggressive behavior in controlling someone as a part of the relationship dynamic.

There are also accidental boundary violations which are an unintentional act that offends someone, such as accidentally bumping into someone or stating an opinion that is in opposition to someone's beliefs.

Just as we all have preferences about food, color, clothing, careers, we also have a varied definition of boundaries.

When my husband and I first moved in together, he was leaving for a business trip and I told him I would pack his suitcase. He got very offended and stated, "I can pack it myself; you're not my mother." Whoa! This took me aback for a moment. I realized it may have been a trigger that I had no idea about. Once we discussed it, he realized I wasn't trying to control him, or dictate what he should bring, or treat him as a child. I was just trying to be a helpful wife. We laugh now, and that boundary is no longer an issue.

If you really look at it, boundaries are sometimes just the triggers that remind us of a past experience that we no longer want to relive. They can also be hard lines drawn based on what you were taught growing up.

I have a boundary when it comes to privacy. My children know this so well that they will never go in my purse even if I tell them to grab something. I don't open my husband's mail, even if it's just junk mail. I would never go through his wallet (even when he says it's fine with him). This boundary was something that I had instilled and programmed from my mother growing up. It stuck with me and I feel it's reasonable.

When in a relationship, what boundaries have you set?

Do you enforce them?

Is the other person aware of them?

These are not rhetorical questions. If boundaries are not communicated, it's difficult to have expectations met. Here are some healthy boundaries that should be observed in every partnership:

1. **My Body, My Decision:** Although we get intimate in relationships, we do not forfeit our right to our bodies, the control of where and how use our bodies, and the comfort level we prefer. In friendships and professional settings, be aware of how others communicate in nonverbal manners. Body language is a key component in identifying someone's boundaries.

    If you observe someone who loves to hug strangers or constantly puts their hand on someone's arm, they are probably quite comfortable in their boundaries of personal space. However, if you see someone crossing their arms, standing sideways, or looking away, they may have more stringent expectations about distance in personal space.

    Listen to the way someone speaks. It will tell you how someone receives information. When you hear a coworker state, "I see how that is," they are a visual person. When your parent says, "I hear what you are saying," they are an auditory communicator. Most importantly, we need to be aware of others and their needs. We can't assume someone's preference, so it's okay to ask, "Are you comfortable if I give you a hug?" The key is respect and clear communication.

2. **Don't Tell Me What to Feel:** I've surveyed several of my women friends and I asked them, "What is the most annoying thing your spouse or boyfriend says when you argue?" This is the overwhelming winner—"I'm sorry *you* feel that way." In other words, we are made to feel like we should be ashamed of our response and that our feelings are not validated.

   If you've ever had an unfortunate rendezvous with an individual who displays narcissistic personality traits, you are probably familiar with the term "gaslighting," where someone convinces you that your reasoning or views are crazy or unfounded. Even people without NPD (narcissistic personality disorder) can twist your feelings or words to confuse you or make you question if you are being reasonable and justified. And others can trigger your fear of conflict or drama by becoming aggressive or hostile.

   While coaching my couple clients in sessions, I emphasize the importance of using "I" statements. For example:

   "I apologize for saying that."

"I realize I caused feelings of... (sadness, anger, frustration)."

"I feel angry because..."

"I would like it if we could spend more time together, have more intimacy, etc." Notice I said "we," not you, as that could be taken as a demand.

In doing this, we validate that the partner was justified in their reaction and we own our part in causing it. It is not okay to tell your partner how they should feel. The key is to listen to the words without defensiveness in order to change the negative feelings or hurt in the other person. In an upcoming chapter, there is a discussion about effective communication in a relationship.

3. **It's My Choice:** There are varying degrees of how much "control" we allow others to have in our lives. From overbearing "helicopter" parents, to spouses who "wear the pants," the amount of control is completely up to you. When we have difficult people in our lives, we tend to allow boundaries to be crossed. The fear of upsetting someone or dealing with the drama is too overwhelming, so we concede.

It's essential that you stick to your limitations. Your best indicator is how you feel. If someone is aggressive or threatening to you, it's a good indication they should not be a priority in your life. Distancing yourself from them would be a healthy option. When setting boundaries in a relationship, the ideal companion will lift, encourage, support, and allow you to be your best self. Allowing space and freedom to do, be, and speak honestly is the gift and unconditional love that should be expected in a healthy union!

4. **Ethically Speaking:** We all have a set of morals, values, and beliefs that we have molded, changed, and perfected throughout our journey thus far. Let's talk about the boundaries relating to the ethical standards we have set for ourselves.

   a) **Lying:** In your childhood home, was it okay to tell a "little white lie" to spare someone's feelings from being hurt? Did your family lie to cover for each other? What level of lying would you consider acceptable? In my home, lying was a big no-no. We were the kids who got soap in our mouths if we lied (or cursed).

   This carried over to my parenting style, where I gave positive reinforcement for truth-telling (without the soap). My daughter Lacee came home from school on a Friday during her fifth grade year. She had a sleepover with her girlfriends planned for that night that she was super excited about. Unfortunately, she had received a note from her teacher stating she had received disciplinary action for something she had done. Instead of waiting until Sunday to give it to me, she handed it to me right after school, at the risk of knowing she would not be able to attend her sleepover. I was really surprised and really proud of this decision. I explained to her that I was disappointed in the note, but I allowed her to go to the sleepover because she was honest about giving me the note, despite being scared she would miss out on her fun night with friends.

b) **Gender Roles:** How was gender equality viewed in your household? Should men and women have specific chores based on gender? What are your expectations of the workload for each partner? My husband and I have a "nothing is your job, nothing is my job" policy. He was the one who presented this to me. In my first marriage, I followed the lead of my own mother. I cooked, cleaned, took care of the kids, and even did the yard work, plus held a full-time job! In relationships to follow, I determined to find a man who would equally share the household responsibilities. It is a personal decision and boundary that each couple can decide. Some couples find complete harmony in assigning duties to each person.

c) **Spiritual and Religious Beliefs:** When you begin to date someone, as discussed previously, compatibility is very important. If your spiritual beliefs are a high priority, then seek to find the same in a potential partner. However, there are couples who believe in the *opposites attract* model. Just be sure to understand that it is not your job to convert anyone to your beliefs.

For example, if you meet someone who is a Christian and you are an atheist, it's not your goal or job to convince them to see things as you do. If this is how you met one another, you accept them as they are and don't aim to change them. Respect that this could affect your relationship once children are involved as well. Communicate what the expectations are for holidays, ceremonies, and daily devotions. Balancing the need to communicate your beliefs without falling into the trap of trying to persuade the other person to change their beliefs is an important part within a successful relationship.

d) **Language of Love:** Have you ever been around a family who drops curse words like reciting a poem? During my childhood, we were not allowed to curse at all. In fact, if a curse word slips out around my parents even now that I'm an adult, I feel like I have disappointed them greatly.

I wasn't that strict with my kids but did require respect when speaking to and around me. Outside of your personal stance on cursing, what are your boundaries for speech? I noticed immediately a difference in the way my husband spoke to me when dating. He was very respectful. He is a very intelligent man and knows the logistics and details of certain things that I don't fully grasp.

At the beginning of our dating, he used a lot of sarcasm and, at times, condescending talk. He didn't do it intentionally; it was something he had done for a lot of years, but I did need to bring it to his attention. He was willing to recognize and change that because it upset me. He would always say, "You need to tell me when I'm doing it."

I found it refreshing and attractive that he was willing to say, "I want to recognize and change that for you." We aren't always aware of how we speak. Sometimes it's just a personality trait or habit, and the assumption is that our partner knows (or accepts) how we speak. That may be true, but it also may not be something they like or enjoy.

I always say, you can't change what you don't know.

In essence, we are not always self-aware or self-actualized to see our own behavior. I respect a partner or friend who brings it to my attention with love. When you are secure, you will view it as helpful. Try not to let any insecurities bring out defensive responses.

What I love the most about my marriage to Dennis is the way we speak to one another. We thank each other for doing everyday chores, we remind one another how blessed we are to be together, and we compliment the traits we love in each other. He has taught me that kindness of words and love through affirmations keep the love and admiration strong in our love connection.

Chapter 13

FRIEND ZONE OR
A FRIEND AT HOME

I envy the simplicity of the view dogs have regarding interactions and relationships with humans and other dogs. There are no levels of relationship when it comes to our canine friends, or within our feline friends. They just decide from the initial meeting how they feel about the new encounter. There is no "friend zone." You are either a friend or a foe. They don't overthink or weigh out options of which way to view it. They go with their instincts. We should do more of this "going with our gut" method. Pay attention right away if something feels immediately like a connection or if something is off. I know this sounds way too simple for the complicated intricacies of humans, but maybe we should just keep it this simple without overthinking and overanalyzing every word and action. Just feel your way through.

If you've ever dated, I'm certain you've had to "friend zone" someone. This is when you like a person and their traits, but you just don't feel chemistry or attraction to them beyond enjoying their company. At times, we really like someone and try to force the next level. IT WILL NEVER WORK! What it does do, though, is add to what I like to call the "paper bag of qualities." The paper bag of qualities is taking pieces of past relationships or people who have qualities you admire, and putting them in the bag to create (or attract) the person you seek to find true love with.

For example, I dated a gentleman who was very giving and kind, but I just didn't "feel it" with him. I took the giving and kindness qualities and put them in the bag. I also dated someone whom I respected for his ability to have long, meaningful conversations with me. Still, I didn't "feel it," but I put *that* quality in my bag. The more I healed from past disappointments and abuse, the more I attracted those with qualities I desired, until finally, my husband came, and he had the "whole bag."

In any case, keep going until your person list (bag) of attributes that you seek in a partner has been fulfilled.

Dogs make friends with a wide variety of people and animals. A dog owner generally sees the way their pet interacts with people and animals and can gauge the "friendship" traits of their dog. You frequently hear dog owners say: "She doesn't like men" or "She loves everyone." Let's review your friendships to analyze the traits you like in a friend. If you were to write down the names of the people in your circle, what kind of assets do they have? Are they good listeners? Are they there when you need help, support, or encouragement? Do you have one-sided friendships, selfish people, or controlling friends? This is a good measurement to let you know if you have some more healing to do. As you heal, you set the vibration or "vibe" for what you will attract.

I will be honest; I am not a person who likes talking on the phone. I prefer person-to-person conversations or even texting. During the 2020 quarantine, I really took things to a new level with not talking on the phone. So much so that my best friend, Linda, texted daily since she was worried about me. She also started to get a complex about whether I was upset with her. Finally, I called her, and I was laughing about it, but she kept saying, "I'm serious, I felt like you didn't care." Nothing had changed for me, but I realized she NEEDED me. She calls it her "Mo fix."

In 2019, I reunited with another friend, Laura, my best friend throughout high school. We picked up right where we left off twenty-five years ago, as though no time had passed. Again, during the quarantine, when I wasn't answering calls, she posted on Facebook and called me out for it. I thought it was hilarious (see, no offense taken) and when I called her, we spoke for three hours.

These two wonderful women (age range over forty-five) have both recently entered into committed relationships after dating for some time. What is interesting to me is that they both stated the same things when starting the relationships. This time they were both healed enough to take things slow and steady. They had no expectations outside of the new partner meeting their bar and maintaining the boundaries they had set for themselves. They both said, "I'm not all giddy like I was in my youth, and I'm just letting it flow to see where it goes." They understood this finally that when you heal, you will attract exactly what you want. Taking the time to enjoy the journey adds to the love story you build.

A slow burn is better than a quick explosion. In other words, just allow the authenticity of the process. There's no need to rush. Don't have unreasonable expectations, let things flow, and see where it takes you. You will know if you are on the right path with the right person. It will feel right organically.

When you stop searching, it will come when you are ready. I believe it's a validation you have met the desire or energy you have by becoming the most whole person you can be. You finally learned the lesson from the experience you asked for. And now you are mindful (self-aware) of what you deserve and want.

As I mention healing quite often throughout this book, I'd like to dissect or clarify more of what the healing means. It is the practice of mindfulness.

Here are a couple of definitions entailing what mindfulness is:

1. the quality or state of being conscious or aware of something.

2. a mental state achieved by focusing one's awareness on the present moment, while calmly acknowledging and accepting one's

feelings, thoughts, and bodily sensations, used as a therapeutic technique.

In the stories above, these women both said the person they are with now is NOT who they would have thought they wanted nor previously sought or found attractive. To me, this reveals that their subconscious mind has developed a much better understanding (or feeling) of what they needed to be fulfilled versus their previous preferences.

One of the key points in a relationship is having a genuine friendship with the person we are with.

I remember dating in my youth, and then again after my divorce, when I was in my thirties. I had no idea what I wanted. I always said, "I want fireworks and fairy tales." What possibly does that mean in reality? I realize now how silly that sounds! I was trying so hard to get someone to love me and to feel that "puppy love" yearning that we feel with our first love. When I was younger, I had not fully learned how to love myself. I would do everything in my power to make sure those I was involved with were happy even when they were not fully giving back to my needs.

In the years since then, I have learned that a relationship HAS to be a give-and-take. This does not mean being argumentative or combative. Like every relationship in life, we should get a satisfaction or fulfillment from being in the union. Unfortunately, a lot of our childhood programming comes into play in our adult relationships and we play the tapes that state,

"If you don't have something nice to say, don't say anything."

My opposing belief is that we are entitled to speak our personal truth, even if it is not nice. That is not to say we shouldn't be respectful and tactful, but we should have the strength and confidence to be candid and honest. Below are some other phrases you may relate to that your parents or grandparents said. They are quite telling about how the mentality of today has changed. These phrases are point-blank and basically do-as-I-say instructions. Thank goodness most people have become more compassionate about child-rearing.

See if you can relate to any of these:

1. Because I said so. (just do what I want you to do, you don't get a say)

2. Stop crying before I give you something to cry about! (translation, don't express emotion)

3. You're not made of sugar, you won't melt. (translation, don't be so sensitive)

4. You'll live. (translation, get over it)

5. You brought this on yourself. (A harsher way of saying you attract what you put out, hello, karma)

6. Can't never did. (You need to try before you declare that you cannot do something. Okay, I kinda like this one as a way of promoting us to just go for it and not make excuses.)

7. Who do you think you are? The Queen of England? (today's version is Yaaaas, Queen)

8. You can, but you may not. (translation, you need my permission)

9. We're not laughing AT you; we are laughing WITH you. (I am certain that this one has instilled many insecurities throughout generations)

10. I suppose you think you are special. (translation, I don't think you're special, and neither should you.)

11. Wipe that smile off your face, or I'm gonna wipe it off for you. (Translation, I want to resort to physical violence to get you to stop making me feel frustrated or insecure.)

12. You kids will be the death of me yet. (Translation, parenting is exhausting and frustrating, and I (the parent) am not afraid to tell you that.)

We know our parents weren't intentionally trying to emotionally stunt our growth, but these phrases certainly weren't confidence building or compassionate. Overall, I think past generations didn't see children as individual thinking and contributing humans, but more like mirror images or carbon copies of themselves. In addition, their children were a reflection of them and their achievement of producing a "good" human being to send out into society. Hence, the "children should be seen and not heard" mantra was common. I am so glad that today's society of parents has learned more about really listening and nurturing our children. Furthermore, embracing the individuality of each child has to happen in order to be the best parent to each child. There is no longer a one-size-fits-all parenting model from generations past.

If you have children or plan on parenting one day, I'd love to instill this one nugget of advice: You are not responsible for your child's success or failure, only the guidance with validation and encouragement that helps them make the most positive choices they can. Yes, the guidance you provide to your children will have an impact on their future. Yes, your example behavior will help them choose the type of partner they seek out. Yes, the self-esteem you help build in your child will affirm their belief in themselves and their worth. Yes, even your mistakes can influence the adult your child will become to either copy or rebel against your example.

These are all very powerful influences, but they are not a guarantee of good behavior or decision making. Parenting is demanding and not a leisure activity for the faint of heart. A parent needs to be determined to send healthy, happy, contributing, respectful, responsible adults into the world, and then consciously make decisions that support the positive outcome we are seeking. It's a constant evolution of learning and changing. Have an open mind to consistently try new ideas and methods. Your partner needs to be a supportive partner in this goal.

The way we pursue our lifelong partners, spouses, and mates has a lot to do with these integrated beliefs we learned as children.

If you are determined to find an amazing partnership, it's important to look at your relationships, marriages, or dating situations, and be sure you are staying focused on valuing your needs and ensuring the relationship is serving to make you the best person you can be.

Be patient when sorting through the dating process. Don't insert an imaginary hope into a reality person. Creating a fantasy of what they could be will not help assess who they really are. You may be setting expectations this new individual cannot meet. When it comes to finding love, you can liken it to buying a car. You do research, you know the color, body style, dependability, and performance you prefer. You go to several dealerships to get the best price and service. It takes some work, but you will end up with precisely what you want in the end. Although the research is not as easy, finding a perfect partner is also a process of looking at the characteristics of the people you date and comparing them objectively to your needs, beliefs, and ideals.

While patience is not a quality that everyone has, in relationships, it is a quality that we all need.

To add to the patience requirement, I think it significant to mention vulnerability. There are many motivational speakers who talk about this subject, and I feel it means something unique to each individual. Here are different aspects and perspectives of what vulnerable can mean.

1. **Having to ask for help, advice, or assistance:** If you have lived alone and have been independent for some time, this one can feel very uncomfortable when beginning a new union with someone. Pride is usually a challenge with this view.

2. **Letting the skeletons out of the closet:** This represents sharing your past. Opening up the doors of past failure, shame, and bad choices. This can be rough as the fear of judgment rears its ugly head. Acceptance of your previous experiences will assist in this view.

3. **Someday:** This is the sharing of hopes, dreams, fantasies, and wishes. This is a person's most vulnerable, deep dark place that only they visit. Inviting another into this private space can be frightening.

4. **To plug or unplug:** It's all about power. Or to be more specific, power struggles. We each have a varied view of how much or how little power we have over our lives. It's about the freedom we seek. Being in a relationship can be seen as "How much power am I willing to give up?" Although skewed, this view is common, and individuals have difficulty giving freely, so they remain guarded to protect themselves. Trust is a key factor in dealing with this view.

What do you think your view is related to vulnerability? Are you an open book? Are you willing to share openly? Do you need years before you are able to? Does your partner have to prove worthy of hearing your vulnerability narrative?

In order to connect on a deeper level with another, getting over the vulnerability hurdles is a must. A relationship cannot survive a superficial, surface interaction for very long. If you are able to fully accept who you are, sharing these vulnerabilities is easy. Confidence and self-esteem are cornerstones to healthy sharing and awareness.

Chapter 14

LET'S TALK ABOUT IT

During the day, Brodie will be lying on the floor taking a nap. Jade loves to come up to him and lick his nose or start playing. He sometimes moans as if to say, "Ugh, right now? I'm trying to sleep." In the morning when I sit outside and start my day, all three pups come out to greet the day. Without fail, Brodie starts a morning howl, with Jade's high-pitched bark and Callie's short little yelp joining in. I'm certain my neighbors roll their eyes and don't enjoy the "song" as much as the dogs and I do. What I love is that even though animals are not verbal communicators, they express themselves in a variety of ways through sounds.

If there is one, all-encompassing, key, vital, crucial, omni-important factor in any relationship, it is good communication. Notice I said GOOD communication, not just communication.

Learning how to effectively translate your partner's needs and vice versa through verbal and nonverbal communication is a critical part of a long-lasting, healthy relationship. Like the ocean, our relationships ebb and flow and change on a consistent basis because we change. Below are some phases of communication based on the stages of a relationship.

1. **Introduction or Who Are You Phase:** This phase is quite obviously about how we introduce ourselves to a new possible love partner. Have you ever gone on a date and spilled everything about you? Or are you so guarded from past hurt that you just do the twenty questions game on the poor victim across the candlelit dinner table? We've all been there, right?

   Early in a relationship, it is tough to know how much information to give at what point. I think it's safe to just shadow what the other person does. If they are very chatty and open, go ahead and share your first grade teacher's name and how your dog, Fido, likes to roll around in the yard. I jest, of course, but it is okay to follow the lead of others and only say what you're comfortable with. You will have time to reveal more if you feel this person is compatible.

2. **Compatibility or You Like, I Like Phase:** This phase explores likes and dislikes. It can reveal a person's moral character, personal beliefs, and goals. For example, a friend of mine went on a first date with a guy for dinner. They had a nice time, had good conversation, and it led to a second date. On the second date, they decided to go hiking.

   As they were hiking, there was no conversation. She attempted to ask questions, but he didn't respond or reciprocate. An older couple approached them, asking how to get to a certain trail. The guy just pointed and said, "I don't know, I think over there." My friend, on the other hand, has a soft spot for the elderly. She wanted to walk with them and show them how to get there, so his dismissiveness of the couple was very off-putting to her.

She realized just two dates in that he didn't have the kindness and compassion she was looking for in a partner. As she told me about the date, she debated whether to go out on a third date. I walked her through a thought process, like I am with readers in this book. I stated, "You've already seen a core piece of his character that isn't compatible with your beliefs. Do you believe that will change?" I asked if she wanted to pursue and spend her energy on this man. She realized then that wasting time with someone who is "not a good fit" doesn't make sense.

3. **Swimming Pool Phase:** This is the phase where we deep dive into who each other really is, and swim around in their world. We start sharing our dreams, wishes, hopes, and fears. This can be a scary phase within a budding relationship. Similar to someone just learning to swim, deep diving into an emotional body of water can be a difficult thing, especially if you've been out of the dating lake for a while.

   This is a pertinent phase that must be faced in order to move to a commitment with someone. It's good to have an idea of what you really want to know. It's also the time to see this person in all aspects of their life. I'm a fan of full disclosure and believe it's fair to each other to see the good, the bad, and the ugly.

I have a friend who explained that at a farmer's market, an apple vendor will put the best apples on the top of the barrel to entice buyers. In comparison, do we, as couples, only show the good apples of ourselves and hide the bruised ones (the less proud points) on the bottom?

Here are some questions to address as you contemplate a relationship with someone:

What is the relationship like with their family?

How do they speak to (or about) their coworkers, exes? children? waitstaff?

What are their plans for the future?

What is their dream vacation?

What is their biggest phobia or fear?

Who is their hero?

What are their plans for retirement? What is their perspective on finances (saver versus spender)?

What were their past relationships like?

Do they have any ownership in the breakup?

How do they view the opposite sex?

What do they think partner roles are in a marriage?

Do they want children? How do they treat your children or their own children?

What are their political views? How do they compare to yours?

Are there financial hardships or struggles that will become yours if you integrate?

These are all questions to consider. If you find the answers don't match with your beliefs or morals, you may want to reconsider moving forward. It is impossible for you to change someone's beliefs or even to see your perspective on many topics.

4. **Transition or Blinker Phase:** This is an interesting phase because it can make or break a union. This is where the rubber meets the road, so to speak.

When my husband, then fiancé, moved into my home, we had to make a lot of adjustments. Let's just say cutting the grass in straight lines or circles around the yard can be a contentious subject.

We found that since we had both lived alone for quite some time, making adaptations seemed to bring many triggers for both of us. It was almost a power struggle at times, as if we had to prove we were the better domestic engineer than the other. I, especially, had to let go of wanting to control every aspect of the home operations. He had to feel that my home was now his home and now equaled our home.

The reason I call it the Blinker Phase is because there are constant twists and turns, and we must learn to stay in our own lane. When we want to make a change, we need to signal that change to our partner, and make sure to communicate not only the What of the change, but also the Why of the change. The nucleus of this phase is understanding.

Communication during this phase is so important because we could easily expect our partner to know what we are thinking. As my husband calls it, "Transparent Expectations"—if they love me, they should know what I am thinking. While that is possible, it is not realistic to expect your new partner to understand you without open and clear communication. This is the stage when you set a precedent for how you will speak to one another and resolve conflict, when you will create the process or methodology for your personal couplehood. Remember to speak as you want to be spoken to. If you consistently come from a place of respect and not command, you will see the best results.

As hard as it may be, it is important to bring attention to specific situations that are highly emotionally charged to integrate what is the most effective solution for both of you. Conflict can be difficult, and certainly the triggers from your past can cause you to put up a wall or run away (emotionally or physically) or just give in to avoid the conflict altogether. Being able to change your response to triggers and talk through challenges will demonstrate growth as a person as well as a couple.

In my experiences with Dennis, we have been able to come up with solutions and compromises without making one another feel undervalued or excluded. The process can be slow and emotional. Communication about how you feel throughout any process or change allows your partner to gain understanding about you. Additionally, seeking knowledge about how your partner is feeling also improves your understanding of them!

For instance, if a previous lover refused to buy new furniture, don't punish your current partner out of the anger a past memory regenerates. It's really about being open-minded and willing to change for the harmony and good of the union. I have benefited greatly from the acceptance of the changes! I no longer go to the grocery store, which I used to despise. I don't have to put gas in my car or take the garbage out. If you let go, you will see how much you can gain.

5. **Committed or Binocular Phase:** When you arrive at this phase, you hopefully have found and are utilizing the tools that are needed for conflict resolution, understanding each another, and adaptation to life's changing events. The Binocular Phase is about envisioning a future with your special someone. Now you are looking toward the future, marriage, possibly children, buying a home, careers, retirement, and growing old together.

You should have the same goals for these long-term visions.

The questions that allow you to successfully be in this phase would have been asked in the **swimming pool** phase. If these intimate discussions have not transpired or have been too shallow before getting to this phase, then it may be premature to consider yourselves ready to be a committed couple. You may find that you have fundamentally different goals and views of the future, which will result in a dysfunctional relationship. Again, I want to reiterate, we can't try to change someone's core beliefs or perspective. If you find someone doesn't want children, but you aspire to be a mom or dad, moving forward would be a very poor decision and one that is unlikely to result in a happy and cohesive relationship.

Every evening, we take the furry babies for a walk. Brodie likes to be in the lead with Jade following close behind. Even if Brodie veers from our normal route, Jade just keeps following him. They are of the same mind-set, and Jade is happy as long as her brother is leading her. In this same way, sometimes our partner does something out of the ordinary. Rather than trying to fight them on the "what" ("What are you doing?"), ask them why ("Why did you do this?"). Diving into their reasons and being open to the discussion will give you a deeper understanding of them as a person. I always say to my husband, "As long as we're doing it together, we're still on the right path."

While these are common phases, each of us will experience them in different ways, and some may be blended together. Your ability to communicate effectively and listen openly will help you figure out as a couple what works best for you both.

Chapter 15

PUT UP YOUR DUKES

*"**Don't fight a battle if you don't gain anything by winning.**"*—Erwin Rommel, one of the most successful German commanders in World War II.

Every afternoon or evening, the pups will go out into the yard and start wrestling, growling, and rolling around trying to dominate one another. It's quite entertaining and hilarious to watch them try to outwit their fluffy siblings. Sometimes one of them gets a little too rambunctious and the other will show some teeth and growl. They aren't aggressive, but they are letting the others know to leave them alone. Similarly, every time I sweep the patio, Callie, the border collie, attacks the broom in an attempt to protect me. Apparently, the broom is a scary threat, just like the vacuum. I have to repeatedly tell her to leave it alone.

This can be the same in our relationships. I believe many men can relate to my poor husband, who, at times, has no idea how to deal with me. A misunderstanding between men and women can be due to a number of reasons: we are hungry, hormonal, fatigued, or even sick. However, sometimes it's a Mars and Venus difference between men and women who don't always understand the reasoning of the other person.

I love a portion of the dialogue between characters in the movie *White Men Can't Jump*, a 1992 movie written and directed by Ron Shelton.

Here is a great example of the different approaches and thoughts between women versus men:

Gloria Clemente: (played by Rosie Perez):

"See, if I'm thirsty, I don't want you to bring me a glass of water; I want you to sympathize.

I want you to say, Gloria, I too know what it feels like to be thirsty.

I too have had a dry mouth.

I want you to connect with me through sharing and understanding the concept of dry mouthedness."

Billy Hoyle's response (played by Woody Harrelson):

"When I say I'm thirsty, that means if anybody in the room has a glass of water, I'd love to have a sip."

Here's how Webster's dictionary describes conflict:

1. to be different, opposed, or contradictory: to fail to be in agreement or accord

    and/or

2. mental struggle resulting from <u>incompatible</u> or opposing needs, drives, wishes, or external or internal demands

Anytime we have a conflict with another person, the underlying emotions include insecurity, embarrassment, anger, shame, guilt, hurt, frustration, and feeling unvalued.

The resulting actions and words are to diminish the pain of these emotions by protecting ourselves.

Conflict is not necessarily a bad thing. It can be viewed as an opportunity to view ourselves from another's view. It can be a way to improve on habits we have acquired that haven't served us well. Consider conflict an obstacle or impasse. We can let it stop us or we can figure a way around or through it. The goal is not to change the other person or their behavior, but to *understand* why they believe or behave as they do, as well as what we ourselves are saying and doing.

Callie, our border collie, is bouncy like Tigger from Winnie the Pooh. When she plays fetch, it's as if she has springs on her feet. Her fetch goals are to catch the ball before it bounces on the ground, so she leaps to meet it in the air. Callie ALWAYS wants to play fetch, and the other two dogs will want to join in occasionally. Then there is the wrestling, running to see who is at the door, and napping space. With three dogs, three adults, and two grandchildren in the house during the COVID-19 quarantine, it proved to be a challenging time for personal space. I noticed that Callie was the only one who was a professional at overcoming the impediments to her path. She hops and leaps over everything. She looks like a prize-winning horse in a fence-jumping competition.

I view any person or situation that is difficult in the same way. Difficult situations or conversations are something we can avoid (procrastination), we can go around (avoidance), or we can leap ahead (determination).

Which of these methods do you practice most often? Your answer will reveal areas which may need some improvement—areas where you need to understand why you approach difficult situations with a specific behavior.

When it comes to conflict or disagreements in relationships, most often we want to be right. We are looking for the agreement from the opposing person to ensure we are validated and accepted. If we know we are intelligent, kind, or lovable, the level of need for being right diminishes.

Here's an example:

> My husband and I tend to disagree about where things are placed in the home. The garage is his domain; however, I get frustrated if things aren't organized, or at least how I see organization! Each shelf (in my opinion) should have a grouping of items in a similar category. Garden stuff should go together, coolers should be in the same vicinity, etc.
>
> One day I was looking for an insulated lunch bag I needed for an outing. I would put this item in the ice cooler section. When I was unable to find it, I blamed my husband for not putting it back. He wasn't helping me look for it either, and stated, "I have no idea where it is."
>
> For a couple of days, it was a splinter under my skin.
>
> My best friend Linda came over for coffee the following morning and said to me, "Oh, I forgot to give you back the lunch bag I borrowed." My mouth dropped

open and I felt so silly for forgetting I had given it to her. With my tail tucked, I called to my husband and explained that I was sorry, and I felt bad for blaming him. Now I COULD have just put it back and never said a thing, but I wanted to do the right thing by showing him I care about his feelings and that I will admit my wrongdoings.

When a couple has a discussion or argument, they both need to avoid escalating the discussion into fighting. The difference between having a conflict and fighting is the level of emotion involved. Fighting will generally not resolve a disagreement within the relationship. Conflict can easily grow into fighting when one or both people treat the other unfairly.

Here is an exercise in conflict communication and resolution I use with my Couples in Coaching, and the rules for being fair and constructive during a discussion:

1. **Discuss one issue at a time:** Address the problem at hand and do not bring up everything your partner has ever done. Each person within a discussion needs to conform to this rule, since drawing other issues into a discussion will only lead to anger and disengagement during the discussion.

2. **No name calling:** Discuss the issue, not the person. Speaking in a derogatory manner is a defense mechanism used to make the person feel as bad as you are feeling. It is also not intended to be constructive by the person doing the name calling; rather it is an attack on the other person. With name calling, the wound heals, but the scar remains. The excuse of "I said it out

of anger in the heat of the moment" does not make it acceptable.

3. **Use "I" statements:** "I feel frustrated" as opposed to "You make me angry." This is an important time to use the method of "speaking your truth."

4. **No running away:** Conflict makes most people anxious. I would call this the flight action in the "fight or flight" response that we all have. Many of our past experiences can trigger this reaction, including domestic violence incidents. In some cases, this is an appropriate response, and I certainly advocate that anyone who is experiencing abuse finds a way to leave that situation and keep themselves and their children safe. In situations where leaving is just an emotional response, it is generally not constructive to slam doors or storm out of the house. This is a situation where you need to communicate your need for space to collect yourself before addressing the conflict.

5. **No stonewalling:** At the beginning of our relationship, when Dennis and I would disagree, I would retreat or say, "I don't want to talk about it." This would frustrate Dennis because he really wanted to work it out right away. He said something each time that would put my guard and defenses down and help me want to work it out. He would say, "I want to try to understand you better." I have learned that silence, or giving someone the cold shoulder, doesn't help the situation and can create frustration in your partner. Rather than just going silent, ask for some time to collect your thoughts

and emotions so that you can have a calm, constructive discussion.

6. **Volume control:** Often when we disagree or argue, we believe the louder we get, the more the person will listen to us. To the contrary, yelling either makes us retreat or try to get louder than the other person. If you find the argument getting louder, stop and state, "Maybe we should walk away and come back to this later." Indicate to your partner that you want to discuss this issue, but that you need time and space to cool down.

7. **Take turns:** We need to ensure we are hearing and being heard. Give your partner time to explain themselves. There could even be a key word when each partner is ready for feedback and feels like they have said their piece. Use words like "go ahead," "I'm finished," "you." Try not to interrupt as this is received by your partner as disrespectful.

8. **Figure out the compromise:** You both can brainstorm and figure out the best way to address the issue if it rears itself up again. Specifically, you could have a word that reminds you or your significant other that "we're doing it again." Like a color, fruit, or celebrity name. It also removes the intensity and relieves the propensity to blame or point fingers.

In addition to getting through the conflict, disagreement, or misunderstanding, reflect on how or why it came up to begin with. After discussing the feelings below, try an exercise where you switch roles and discuss the disagreement as if you were the other person. This helps us to see things from another's perspective.

9. **The Oreo Effect:** This method is great for not only a love connection, but for family members and business as well. The premise is this: the top cookie is how you open the conversation. Use positive words such as, "I think you are amazing, and I know you are sensitive to others' feelings." DO NOT add the word BUT. By adding the word "but," it negates the affirmations that were just given. Instead, use AND. "I think you are amazing, and I can see why you did that..." The cream in the cookie is constructive criticism or speaking your truth. "I felt hurt when it was said that I wasn't listening." The bottom cookie is again closing with a positive reinforcement. "I know that we will do better, and I appreciate your willingness to try."

You are the one in control of your feelings. When describing your feelings, it is important to avoid stating, "You made me feel..." Instead, you should indicate how YOU feel, using the simple "I feel..." or "I felt..." Here are some words that can be used to describe your feelings for your companion and for your own self-reflection:

defensive	hurt	criticized
unheard	overwhelmed	angry
sad	misunderstood	worried
alienated	inflexible	unsafe
afraid	tense	out of control
frustrated	morally justified	unattractive

stupid	like leaving	unloved
powerless	stubborn	lonely
like I wanted to win	my opinion didn't matter	
taken for granted	I wasn't feeling liked	

Furthermore, each partner can journal things they recognize about themselves. Sometimes we don't recognize triggers until they happen. I recall once I had an important situation to discuss with my husband about something that happened with my daughter that day.

I called him at work and said, "I have to talk to you about something when you get home." When he arrived home, he was acting odd. He seemed "off" for some reason. I proceeded to tell him about my day and the situation, and he responded with resounding relief. I was so confused. Little did I know that was a trigger for him. Apparently, that is the statement that most of the women in his past used prior to a breakup with him. I felt so bad for him. I obviously had no idea the significance of this statement, but now I make sure to explain WHAT I will be talking about.

Emotions can come out of nowhere and you can ask yourself, "Why did I feel like that?" "Where did that reaction come from?" and even "Why did that upset him/her?"

In a recent course I completed, I learned how to do Cognitive Diffusion. This is the ability to separate a particular incident in the present moment by detaching from the thoughts from the past experience in order to view it (and react to it) differently.

If you've spent time with someone—including family and friends—you begin to learn what their "buttons" are. Those are words that match the emotional response that annoys, angers, and frustrates a person.

Just like voicing the words "park" or "treat" will surely get an excited, energetic reaction from our dogs, the non-constructive verbiage you use with others will get a reaction as well.

What if in your relationship it seems you are always arguing about little things? If you find you are doing this, it's most likely not about the "little" thing; it's a buildup of resentments that are now sitting like an elephant in the pit of your stomach. Time to do some emotional inventory and see where your emotions are coming from.

The chart below is similar to the chemistry periodic table and relates to human emotions, with two-letter abbreviations for various emotions in the categories that our emotions fall into:

LOVE: EM-empathy, SE-serenity, TE-tenderness, CO-compassion, SY-sympathy, GR-gratitude, TS-trustfulness, AD-admiration, PR-pride

JOY: HO-hope, SU-surprise, ST-satisfaction, PL-pleasure, EC-ecstasy, EN-enthusiasm, EA-ease, OP-optimism, EU-euphoria, DE-desire, HA-happiness

ANGER: BM-bad mood, RB-rebellion, HS-hostility, RE-resentment, HT-hate, FR-frustration, RA-rage, JE-jealousy, EV-envy, AR-arrogance, CT-contempt, DI-disgust

SADNESS: BO-boredom, LN-loneliness, AB-abandonment, DC-discouragement, NO-nostalgia, BL-blame, DS-disappointment, WE-weariness, PE-pessimism, ME-melancholy, SB-submission, RS-resignation

FEAR: NE-nervousness, DR-dread, SH-shy, IN-insecurity, SS-stress, CF-confusion, SP-suspicion, TR-terror, SM-shame

To end this chapter about conflict, it's important to discuss the mechanics of the argument, and not just the emotions and communication:

WHO and WHAT: Do you have family members who thrive on knowing your business? Love to give their two cents' worth? Friends who give unsolicited advice? When you have a disagreement with your partner, it is very important to keep it between the two of you. Don't call your BFF and get into a husband-bashing session. I know you want a sympathetic ear, but this is not positive, constructive behavior. Your outward statements about your relationship should show as much restraint as when it comes to posting your life on social media. Be respectful to both your relationship and yourself. Your privacy is a valued treasure, so be sure to protect it!

WHERE: If you're at a family holiday, it is not the time to get into your husband's lack of sex drive! A busy restaurant isn't the time to discuss why your boyfriend hasn't proposed in five years! If an argument ensues while out on a double date, don't ask for input, as surely, the women will team up and the men will have one another's back. No one wins. If you want some help on figuring out what to do, couples life coaching or online resources for conflict resolution can help. This way it will be objective information.

WHEN: Just as important as who is around and where you are, the WHEN to discuss discord is uber important. When your mate comes home from a stressful day and starts telling you about a coworker dispute, it's probably not the time to ask him why he never listens to you!

If your wife has spent the day listening to children fight and cleaning up, when she sits down is probably not the time to tell her to stop shopping online. She won't see this as constructive; rather it is likely to be viewed as another attack on her. The best time to discuss anything meaningful is during the relaxing moments you spend as a couple. You will be more apt to please the other person rather than engage in a dispute. Emotions will be weighing heavier on the pleasure side, so defenses will be lower. If these moments are too few and far between, and you feel you are always waiting to be able to discuss an issue, try to plan more alone time with your partner. This in itself could be the reason for the uncomfortable feelings you are connecting often enough to share openly and honestly.

An argument starts with disagreement and a differing of opinions. Strong viewpoints turn discussions into arguments. The language used can either create or resolve the conflict.

During conflict resolution, the bottom line is that you are both on the same team and fighting for the same prize: a life of joy, peace, connection, and love together. The only way to get better at it is to practice it with patience and understanding of one another.

Chapter 16

IF IT'S NOT ON SOCIAL MEDIA, IT DIDN'T HAPPEN

Those who know me have heard me preach about the importance of nurturing relationships. Today's social media craze social distanced us long before the pandemic ever did. In fact, while we are forced to be apart, I have made an odd observation: We go to social media and post the most real and mundane parts of our lives. This contrasts with how we typically have displayed our lives and emotions to the world and sometimes how we interact with the most meaningful people in our lives, including our spouses and partners.

Real isn't just showing "our best life" or the "perfect" moments. Instead, mundane is being real!

I've seen less selfies and more family photos. Less filters and more outreach. I'm really enjoying this new norm. The positivity I see now is far outweighing the negative of showing the superficial part of our life. I see new groups forming to help others in need, to create ideas to entertain our children while they are not able to attend school, as well as funny memes to make one another smile. Gone are the displays of self-importance or flaunting status or travel destinations that only state: "Look at ME!" I love it when something good is discovered during challenging moments.

My grand doggy Bexley, a red border collie owned by my middle child, Jordania, is so photogenic. For Christmas this year, I bought my daughter an attachment for her phone that holds a ball above the photo lens. Being that Bexley is obsessed with balls, she stares intently at the camera (okay, ball) and my daughter snaps the best photos. Bexley also has her own Instagram page with more followers than I could ever hope for my business page to receive! Yes, the pups are also involved in social media on a daily basis!

Let's talk about what the Internet and social media contribute in a positive way:

1. **Networking:** It is great to be able to make connections with others who are like-minded but whom you would never cross paths with in daily life. Being able to boost one another and promote and support each other to lift and contribute to one another's dreams and goals is amazing.

2. **Building self-esteem:** Sometimes it's nice just to be acknowledged. Social media can help to get engagement from others. Receiving input or affirmations boosts our self-esteem. Although, of course, we need to be sure to avoid any negative forums, statements, or drama. You will get what you give, send positive, get positive. Let's be honest, no one is interested in the stalkers, despite

their compliments. Don't engage with anyone who isn't of the same mind-set that you are. Getting into an online dispute with a complete stranger does nothing for either party. The opposite occurs and then your mind is flooded with ways to get revenge and have the better comeback. There are no winners. Just stay in your lane and don't worry about anyone else.

You are in competition with no one. You are here to do what you alone chose as your path. You created the values that align with the decisions and behavior you embrace.

You can learn from others but don't let the success of others trigger any insecurities of incompetence in you. I recently saw a quote by Roy Goforth that really resonated with me: "There are two types of people who will tell you that you cannot make a difference in this world: those who are afraid to try and those who are afraid you will succeed."

Let the haters be the fuel to your success explosion, not your self-doubt.

3. **Connecting with past and present friends:** Although it's not as important as a person-to-person encounter, social media helps you connect with friends you've lost contact with or haven't heard from or seen in years! I was able to reconnect with most of my high school and grade school friends on Facebook. We also took conversations offline and I learned what people actually thought about me when we were in school (all positive stuff ☺).

Recently, a good friend of mine from high school reached out via messenger. We were able to clear the air about what happened to cause our friendship to fall apart. We picked up right where we left off. I am so grateful to have her back in my life, now as adult women able to love and support one another.

I read a story about a couple who were traveling separately twenty-five years earlier, and they had a great conversation on a train. They arrived at their destination and soon went about their separate lives. They each went on to have marriages, children, and even divorces. By the magic of the Internet, a mutual friend was friends with each of them, and they saw one another's profiles. They were able to reunite and even get together for coffee, not knowing they lived in the same town! They are now happily married to one another. There are a million of these positive stories that are a result of social media.

4. **Soak it up:** I am a huge advocate for learning something new each day! The Internet has made it so convenient for us to learn new content, even the smallest feat or notion, such as learning a new quote. We can take online courses, participate in webinars, have meetings and videos live so that we can interact with others from the comfort of our homes. This technology has opened the door to knowing and doing everything we want to do and be.

I set goals for myself to take at least three classes per year and get additional certification to help my clients.

I love to learn, and when it's something that piques my interest, it doesn't feel like work. I soak it up like a sponge because it is moving me in the direction of my dreams and serving my purpose. Take advantage of how blessed you are to live in these times! You have opportunities your ancestors could have only dreamed of!

Social media is a tool, one that can be used, and certainly one that can be misused. Our engagement with social media can be a positive in our relationships (maintain friendships), or a negative (stalking ex-partners and obsessing about their current relationship). I strive to keep social media as a positive part of my life, rather than allow it to BE my life.

Chapter 18

YOU ARE SPEAKING MY LANGUAGE

L<u>ove</u> **languages** are defined as verbal and nonverbal communications between couples which improve the mental and physical well-being of both partners. These mutual expressions and actions help to build up a nurturing environment in which couples can improve both their emotional and physical intimacy levels.

The love languages are drilled down into five types:

Words of Affirmation: These are verbal expressions of care and affection. They include compliments and words of appreciation. In contrast, insults and name calling can be especially upsetting for those whose primary language is this.

Receiving Gifts: This language includes receiving tangible (flowers) and intangible (gestures) gifts that make a person feel loved and appreciated. For those who favor this love language, the absence of everyday gestures or a missed special occasion can be particularly hurtful.

Acts of Service: This language is about helping and supporting your partner; contributing through services to relieve a partner's burden or show caring. For someone with this love language primary, their partner being dismissive or ambivalent would be very negatively impactful.

Quality Time: For those who love this language, watching a movie together, going on a picnic, or taking a walk would be valuable to their well-being. Partners who are distracted or distant would be detrimental to someone with a primary love language such as this.

Physical Affection: To some degree, we all need and crave physical affection, but those with this love language as primary need the extra cuddles, touches, and kisses. Withholding these or using them as a tool would feel like abandonment to someone with this preference.

Even our furry creatures establish different love languages.

Brodie, our Aussie, is not a big cuddler (physical affection). He doesn't come over and lie on my lap, he doesn't lick my hand or my face, and he isn't even a huge fan of hugs. He is a dog that only needs a little amount of physical affection. As he has aged, he has developed some hip dysplasia and has a difficult time getting up the stairs. He waits at the bottom of the stairs whining for me to come and watch him. I stand at the top of the stairs encouraging him to come up, as I tell him what a good boy he is (words of affirmation). Even as difficult as it is, he wants to be near me at all times (quality time). And yes, he likes his treats too (receiving gifts).

To find out which love language you favor, there are a multitude of quizzes available online. Taking the time to understand your love language will help you to communicate your needs to your partner. In addition, take a quiz with your partner so you can meet their love language as well.

Many couples run into issues when the love language isn't being spoken. Let me explain why. We all tend to give what we THINK the other person needs. Unfortunately, we also tend to give our partner the same love language that we prefer, rather than listening and observing what their language is. YOU may prefer someone mowing the lawn for you (act of service), but your spouse needs to be intimate or kiss (physical affection). We need to communicate what our preference is and ask our sweetheart the same.

You will find that you have a desire for a portion of each language. I've discovered that my husband provides segments of each attribute, and now I've come to desire each one depending on what my need is or how I'm feeling. If I'm tired and he picks up dinner on the way home, that is a wonderful act of service. If my feet hurt after a long day, he gives me a foot rub (physical affection). My primary language is acts of service, but certainly I value several love languages.

Let's dig a little deeper into WHY you prefer a particular method of how love is conveyed. It isn't a superficial need that you suddenly decided in a relationship. It is another programmed learning that we receive throughout our lives. The experiences you have engrain the needs you develop. Here are some examples:

Perhaps while you were growing up, your parents were

not expressive with love. You can't remember hearing "I love you," "You're special," or "You can do it." Your father was focused on good grades, following rules, and being a success. As an adult, you are likely to:

1. Love to hear words of affirmation, crave constant validation and someone to cheer you on,

   Or

2. Believe that actions speak louder than words (acts of service love language),

   Or

3. Be very touchy-feely. You always express your love through words and touch because it was something you lacked in your childhood, and you give this to others to make them feel loved.

Our beliefs can go many ways, but generally we are influenced by what we have lived and witnessed. Those early and fundamental experiences create the belief system and generally the love language that we desire.

Practice Exercise:

What love language was most displayed in your home?

What do you think your partner desires most? (you may be surprised once you do the quiz)

What love language do you give most often?

What love language is a priority for you?

Take the quiz and compare it to your partner and also your children's love languages for extra knowledge.

Chapter 19

So Far, So Good

Every evening when we walk the dogs, Brodie takes the lead and Jade follows behind, sometimes actually walking under his tail. If Brodie gets too far ahead, Jade will pull on the leash until we are caught up with Brodie, and then she will not leave his side for the remainder of the walk. She HAS to be near her big brother. On the flip side, if Jade is too far behind, Brodie will stop, look back, and wait for her. It's so sweet to see how much they love to be near one another.

Brodie is the caretaker of the puppy clan in our house. I believe he wishes there were one of him for every person. It's interesting to see where he will be lying next. Although he prefers to be with me, when my grandchildren are visiting, I take a backseat. He will position himself in the most central place he can find to watch each and every member of the family, as well as his little sister, Jade. If we're outside, he's outside. If I take a nap or at night, you'll find him at the side of the bed between the door and the bed to fend off intruders. I always say he has the ears of a bat, since he barks anytime someone walks by the front of the house.

He is always nearby, and that gives both of us great comfort in our relationship.

Without a doubt, one of the most difficult strains on a relationship is long distance. Whether voluntarily or involuntarily, trying to stay connected when not in the physical vicinity of a loved one is challenging. Time is our most precious resource, and time together is one of the most fundamental aspects of a successful relationship.

Maintaining a relationship over long distance can be done successfully, but the couple must be committed to staying together and in touch.

My first husband and father of my three children was a man I met in high school. We started dating after high school, and he joined the Army once we were married. At the time we were married, it was during Desert Storm, or the war in Iraq. My fellow army wives had husbands who were in infantry battalions and would leave for weeks and months at a time. Fortunately, my ex-spouse didn't get called to do that at the time. The key for those wives was keeping busy. They would focus on their children or join support groups with other wives. Technology wasn't like it is today. Video chats and phone calls make a lot of difference in staying connected.

When it comes to dating someone long distance, although I know it can work, I personally do not recommend it. It may seem fun at first, but as the feelings grow, so does the frustration of being at a distance, the lack of physical contact, and the inability to integrate into one another's lives.

Because I am an advocate for dating someone for a full year before committing to marriage, my belief is that you should experience someone in every situation in order to discern who they really are.

If you find yourself in a long-distance relationship, here are some tips to figure out how to make it work best. Please consider that at some point, when you are finally in the same space, it will be a new starting point no matter how often you've been connecting via distance.

1. **Be realistic:** Don't get caught up in the fantasy. This type of relationship will have extra challenges than those that are more conventional. If you've had positive interactions with your love interest and you feel a connection and believe it's possible to one day have a committed love affair with the person, then it's time to face the reality of what's next. Is it a possibility to integrate your lives? What compromises and sacrifices are each of you willing to give? What are the expectations of each partner? Where will you live? These are very important questions, so don't assume it will all work itself out.

2. **No contact is no connect:** When there's a distance between people, things can easily be miscommunicated or misconstrued. Text messages, phone calls, and videos don't allow us to feel each other's energy, see body language, or clearly hear voice inflection. Trust is key in these liaisons. Self-confidence and security must be strong in each counterpart. Meeting up in frequent intervals is beneficial to learn about quirks and habits, and develop good communication and honesty. This can be a financial burden as well, but it's an investment in your future.

3. **Set a time limit:** All couples have a unique approach to what works for their personal situation. What works for some would be appalling to others.

    I once worked at a restaurant where I met an adorable older couple—regular customers who came in each day for dinner. They had both been married and were widowed. They met each other at a senior center and really hit it off. They continued to live in separate residences but met up every day. They had been implementing this for ten years, and both were very content with the arrangement.

    Perhaps it was their years lived or that they just wanted companionship, but it worked for them.

    In the same way, it is up to the individuals to decide what they want. If you want more of a committed union, set a goal for when you will take the leap and move closer to your long-distance lover. If you are okay with seeing your lover sporadically, then that is something for discussion and mutual agreement.

4. **Don't keep a "someday" mentality:** Although it's good to hope and dream, it's important to focus on the now. Long-distance relationships tend to keep us in the someday mentality because we start to believe everything will be better when "that day" comes. If your days are spent trying to pass time and not fully embracing each day with fun and joy, you might want to reconsider leaving a relationship that doesn't bring fulfillment every single day. Don't hold off on happiness. You may want to seek coaching to understand

why you aren't in need of more commitment (if the separation isn't involuntary, that is.)

5. **Control:** Long-distance relationships remind me of an article I read about women who seek relationships or marry men in prison. This is called hybristophilia in psychological terms. I'm not saying there's anything wrong with this; again, we all have our choices and preferences. But why is this type of relationship ideal for certain women?

   According to Sheila Isenberg, author of *Women Who Love Men Who Kill*:

   "These are women who've been hurt. And when you're in a relationship with a man in prison, he's in prison. He's not going to hurt you. He can't hurt you. So, you're always in a state of control because you're the one who's on the outside.

   You're free.

   You go in and you visit him.

   You can decide whether to accept his collect phone calls.

   So in a way, even though cons are very manipulative—that's why we call them con men and they are manipulative with the women—it's still up to the woman to decide how far she wants to go and she knows she can't be hurt. And every single woman I interviewed had been abused in the past and that's what I found out. That was the big secret."

I went through a period of dating online and only speaking to men (not actually dating) who were located out of state. I was trying to heal (note that I *wasn't* healed yet) from the past hurts from previous relationships, and I was adamant I did not want a relationship. I just wanted friends and occasional companionship. I wanted the attention, but I wasn't ready for the emotion.

I grew emotionally and left that phase of my life. However, if a person isn't able to grow and connect with themselves and realize they deserve much better, they will be content with these types of limitations. Long-distance relationships are a way to postpone relationship growth indefinitely. If possible, you should limit the time in one, or avoid them altogether. By avoiding this detour, you can seek an emotionally and physically available person to connect with and love.

Chapter 20

WHATCHA WANNA DO?

In a little basket in my living room, there are toys and stuffed animals. Each day, I will find a different one in the yard, on the floor, even in another room. It makes me giggle because the puppers have their choices and need stimulation to maintain their happiness. Just like a relationship, they like to "mix it up" with some variety in their day-to-day routines.

The dogs need variety, and so do you and your partner. Since all romantic relationships begin with a date, I thought it would be a fun chapter to contribute some fun and creative date ideas! These range from basic to wacky and outrageous, but I thought I'd give you some variety to choose from and see how adventurous you can be.

We'll start by putting these into date categories:

Romantic: Proposals, anniversaries, birthdays...every couple wants that epic and memorable date or moment to look back on. Here are some ideas for the biggies.

1. Travel to an extraordinary place, somewhere more secluded. Hawaii has all of these attributes, and you can find many places within this beautiful state to enjoy romantic moments, sunset cruises, and even proposals at the top of a volcano.

2. You could go to the place you first met and arrange to have family, friends, and staff meet there as a surprise celebration.

3. A night under the stars whether camping or lying in the back of a truck bed. Bring candles, food, and send off Chinese lanterns.

4. Write a love letter about your story and have it read in public, like at a baseball game, on a plane, or in the middle of a concert.

5. Create an "I found you, now you find me" scavenger hunt. Send your partner to their favorite restaurant, store, city, lake, or campsite, while leaving clues and gifts at each location. Have someone assisting to let you know where they are until the final destination, where you can propose or do a grand romantic gesture.

6. Involve your family, pets, or children. You can send your love to each person and have them give a rose until the bouquet is complete.

7. Go to a winery or brewery where you can make your own bottle of alcohol and you can open it on your one-year anniversary.

Relaxing and Spiritual: When you need to get away from the pressures of life and recharge your batteries and connect as a couple:

1. Take a trip to somewhere with spiritual meaning such as Bali, Indonesia, Peru, Tibet, or Thailand. Research the history and visit those sacred mountains, temples, and archaeological sites.

2. Visit a weekend spa retreat and walk a labyrinth. Get massages together and do some couples or sound meditation sessions.

3. Get out in nature, go hike or camp.

4. Visit haunted or historical hotels.

5. Drive to the ocean and sleep on the beach.

6. Give your partner a "pamper" day. Draw them a bath, give a massage, bring breakfast in bed.

Adventurous: Go do something you've never experienced before. Face and conquer any fears, like heights or physical challenges.

1. **Check off that bucket list!** Go skydiving, even if it's an indoor skydive. Arrange for a glider flight (I have done this, and it is so amazing). For the faint at heart, try a balloon ride or find a flight simulator that gives the essence of flying. Try tandem bungee jumping; you will be hugging each other as you plummet to the ground. That's trust and bonding at its finest.

2. **Let's do this**! Do a mud run, bubble run, marathon together. You can train together and support each other up until the big race!

3. **Water fun:** Go river rafting! Try parasailing, kayaking, caving, or spelunking. Caving means to explore, survey, and document the caves, and the main purpose is the accumulation of knowledge. Spelunking is the visit of caves without any kind of justification; it's the touristic visit of caves. Have a pool day just relaxing or doing laps, or make a race out of it. See who can hold their breath the longest. Have a conversation under water. Play water volleyball or try synchronized swimming with your partner.

4. **Nature, baby!** Go visit animal preserves. Do some birdwatching. Visit a planetarium or natural history museum. Go fishing together. Volunteer to bathe an elephant, feed a monkey, or snuggle baby lemurs. Look in your area or research for a trip.

5. **Move it, move it!** Take dancing lessons together! Make it even more fun and choose different genres like hip-hop, jazz, swing, and even ballet. Join a gym or a spin class as a couple. Make a TikTok dance video. Two left feet? That's okay—it's all about the fun of learning together.

Wacky and Unusual: These are out-of-the-box ideas for some fun and laughter. ☺

1. **Themed dates:** Pick a theme, go to thrift stores, and set a time limit to find your costume or theme. For

example: Find an outfit your grandfather would wear to your graduation or one that looks like a leprechaun. What you would wear for your wedding if it was in the 1950s? Visit a vintage record store and pick your top five favorite albums from your teen years. Plan a trip to places that begin with a letter (like Austin, Abilene, Amarillo).

2. **Rock n roll:** Go to a gem and mineral store and pick out stones for one another. Take a class on gold mining. Join a meetup group to go rock hounding. Learn about rock tumbling. Paint some rocks together. Design a rock garden in your yard.

3. **Cleanup, aisle 2:** Go to a grocery store, set a price and time limit, and come up with the most creative purchases for your partner and for your date. This could be a candle, chocolates, and wine. Or lobster tails and steak. You could be even more creative and find food coloring or fabric dye and make matching tie-dyed shirts.

4. **Sweets:** Find a bakery where you can bake and/or decorate desserts. Take a cooking class together or have a friendly contest at home, each cooking the same meal and judging the best result.

5. **Get me out:** Make a challenge to visit an escape room in every city or once a month. Take pictures then create an "Escape Room Memoir" to relive the moments.

6. **Fabulous, darling:** Give each other a makeover. Style hair differently and pick out clothes (or even lingerie); the other person can't look until the look is complete.

7. **Get down and dirty:** Go to a plant nursery and plant a garden together. Remodel a closet or refurbish and add a new coat of paint to a flea market find.

8. **Find a cause:** Volunteer at a cause that you can support together. Dog rescues, DV awareness, Alzheimer's, anything that is near and dear to you both.

9. **Compete:** Create an "Amazing Race" with other couple friends. The first to arrive wins a prize; the losers buy dinner for everyone.

10. **What's cooking:** Find a restaurant that serves unusual food that neither of you have tasted. Try something outside of your comfort zone, like rattlesnake, eel, or crawfish.

11. **Yikes!** Find out your partner's biggest fear and help them face it with love and support. For instance, if your love is scared of snakes, go to a zoo and look at them, then see if you can have them hold one. Your partner is fearful of heights, maybe try ziplining to help them through it while having fun. Do a tandem bungee jump and get through it as a team.

12. **Mission possible:** Make a list of things your sweetheart can do, and you list a reward for each one. They can choose which ones they want to complete. Example: smash a pie in your face; climb a tree and proclaim your love for your partner by shouting it out loud; approach a stranger and ask for a random item (lipstick for men or a condom for women).

13. **Unplugged:** How about a day with no electronics or technology? Plan a day playing board games or writing a song together. Paint or do something crafty. Put a puzzle together while listening to music. Make music together if you have those talents.

Adventure, creativity, fun, and togetherness create opportunities for bonding and memories. They also give a couple an opportunity to get outside of the routine of taking care of chores and the other aspects of life that aren't as rewarding. Events and adventures also allow us to free emotions and see our partner experience challenges and success in areas that may be outside of their past experiences.

Chapter 21

WHY SHOULD I TRUST YOU?

When it comes to trust, animals are far superior and have an innate ability to forgive far better than we humans. If they could speak, I am certain that we could learn so much from them. Every shelter animal who finds a forever home just trusts that they will now be safe and loved. Even after some of the most horrendous abuse, they are able to let the past go and believe in what's now their present condition. Like us, they may still have reservations, but it's the willingness to trust again that shines through.

When I take Brodie to the groomer, I always feel so guilty. He lets me put the leash on, gets into the car, goes through the building's door, and lets a stranger take him from me. He TRUSTS that I will be back. He trusts that I wouldn't leave him or abandon him.

Imagine this. Your family takes you from your home. No explanation. They just say, "Come on, let's go." They take you to a strange place, introduce you to a stranger, and tell you to go to them.

Would you go willingly?

Would you fight?

Would you believe your family loves you?

Would you believe they were coming back?

Despite how scary this scenario is, animals are consistently in this situation, and we expect them to submit and trust. This is the amazing and sweet nature of our beautiful creatures.

I posted a poll on my Facebook page about this subject. Here are some interesting results:

1. **Which is more important in a relationship, trust or respect?**

   The overwhelming majority of respondents stated they go "hand in hand." One of the best responses stated: "Respect and Trust are mutual, just make it one word: Truspect." Another participant responded, "Trust cannot be a goal in and of itself, as it must be earned daily with respect and honesty." An additional respondent stated, "I tend to trust first so respect and keeping the trust." While still another stated, "If you have respect for someone, trust should be a byproduct of that."

   These responses validate that from our own perspective and experience comes the prioritizing of trust versus respect. In my own experience, it took me a while to realize that I must respect someone in order to trust them.

2. What are the top three things needed in a relationship?

The most common answer was overwhelmingly the need for communication. Facebook responders also alluded in a variety of ways to the need to listen and be present. A close third was the need for laughter and humor. In addition, someone listed adventure, which I wholeheartedly agree with. I loved the following response: "Growth—understanding your relationship is always growing." That translates to the ability to address issues and figure out the best way to work through them.

3. **What does trust mean to you in a relationship?**

The consensus among the sixty-five comments was that trust means "having my back." Here are the related comments:

"Knowing that there won't ever be something done behind my back."

"...self-evaluating on a regular basis is key."

"Trust means being able to rely on your partner when you need it, also to trust or know that person will always be there in your easy and difficult times."

"...that I can go to that person without judgment and they give me no reason to doubt them."

"...partner has my back 100%." I asked him to elaborate, and he stated, *"Actions speak louder than words. To be able to talk and achieve day-to-day tasks and struggles is key to a relationship."*

"Never having to question the love for one another. All-encompassing."

"Trust to me means safety, security, and peace of mind."

"My trust that my husband always has my back. He can call me out for something that he disagrees with. I might not always like it, but I trust he always has his family first no matter what. I can trust in him to make the right choice for us at that time. He can trust me to do the same!"

In summation, we can all agree that it's a fusion of respect and trust that is most important in our relationships in addition to love.

Let's put the love puzzle together even further, it's a cause and effect continuum. When I trust someone, I have respect that they value me and the honesty in our relationship. I value communication and with that communication and openness, I can be confident that my partner has my back.

It's simple. Like choosing a seven-layer dip for our snack—everyone's choice of layers is different, yet we are all trying to fulfill our basic human need to be loved and accepted fully for who we are.

Can trust be restored once lost? Are there hindrances to obtaining or achieving trust? Absolutely to both!

Did your parents ever say trust is easily given but harder to get back once lost? My mother used to say that, and in my youth, I thought it was just another saying. As an adult and having experienced being betrayed in a relationship, I definitely learned what she meant.

When my ex-husband and I were attending AA and Al-Anon meetings for his addiction, we met a couple who would become our sponsors. They seemed very knowledgeable and well on the way to recovery of their marriage. We had moved and I met with the gentleman a few years later. He and his wife were now divorced, and I was really surprised! He explained that he is still sober and runs a recovery center; he has spirituality and has completely changed his life. That being said, of course I asked why they were no longer together, and he said, "She could never fully get that trust back." So even in the best of circumstances, like Mom said, trust is even harder to get back.

I would hate to write a self-help book and leave you on any subject feeling hopeless, so let's continue on this subject. How do I get trust back for someone once I've been betrayed, and how do I earn trust back when I've done the betrayal?

The simple (sorry, not sorry) answer is this—honesty!

Let's look at an analogy:

> There are three doors in front of you. The first door is black, and you hear growling sounds and screams coming from behind it. The second door is red and is slightly cracked open. The third door is made of glass. Which door are you most likely to choose?

> The third door, correct? Why? Because it is transparent, you can see through to the other side, and there are no surprises or anxiety associated with it. You KNOW what to expect.

This is exactly how it works when trying to restore trust. We and our partner must be transparent; we must know what to expect as well as set our own expectations. The truth may not always be comfortable, but it will instill the certainty of openness that is needed to rebuild any loss of feeling you can believe in and count on your partner.

Remember that there will be reminders and triggers connected to this process. It is not an overnight fix. Be patient with one another and yourselves. Acknowledge the challenges.

For instance, if a spouse had an affair, the couple is working through it to rebuild the trust, and the betrayer goes to the store. At the store, the lines are long, he/she goes to another store, needs to stop at a gas station, and takes longer than expected. When the betrayer goes home, the injured spouse instantly questions the amount of time it took and wonders what the betrayer was up to. This is the cycle that will prevent the growth.

Here is an exchange that could help to build the trust:

IS (injured spouse) - Where were you?

B (betrayer) - I was at the store like I told you I would be.

IS - It took a long time. I don't know that I believe you. I don't trust you after what you've done to me…

(Here's the turning point where this discussion could go either way, right? Can you hear the defense weapons being loaded?)

Healthy relationship-rebuilding conversation:

B - I can understand why you feel that way. I apologize that my actions have caused this mistrust and I appreciate that you are willing to try. I will be patient and understand that it will take time for me to earn your trust back.

IS - I recognize that there are going to be times I am triggered from the past hurt. I will work to stay focused on today and not the past. I appreciate that you will understand when these questions come up.

Crisis averted, And...cue the hug.

When we try to see the other person's perspective and put ourselves in their shoes, it helps diminish our own defensiveness in the moment. It also lets the person know they are being heard, which will soften their increased emotions such as anger, hurt, and sadness. It is not only something to use in your romantic relationships but should be integrated into all your relationships that have any form of conflict.

Chapter 22

It's My Culture, You Wouldn't Get It

I recently completed an accredited course in Animal Psychology. I did not enroll in the class to do anything spectacular, like translate a dog's bark to the English language. In all honesty, I wanted to find out why my cat, Grayson, stares at me so often. And why he randomly nibbles (okay, bites) my fingers and toes.

I'm not a deep intellect in my reasoning, but I did learn something interesting as I was listening to the instructor explain the stages of our animals' lives. For example, a dog is considered a puppy until the age of eighteen months. After that, they are considered adolescents up to three years old. Three to six years of age is considered adulthood, while dogs six years and over are considered seniors.

This was new information to me.

Poor Jade just lost three years of adulthood and was catapulted into senior dog territory just because I decided to take a class that would decipher cat stares for me. Sorry, Jade. Curiously, the instructor would condition the stats with "depending on the breed." Even within the canine existence, there are conditions depending on genetics.

This gave me a revelation. Even though we are all humans, there are subcategories of our cultural backgrounds. Not that this was news to me, but I thought it would be important to break down views of love and relationships from a cultural standpoint.

My husband and I were recently watching a wonderful documentary on Netflix called *Sex and Love Around the World*. A CNN journalist named Christiane Amanpour traveled to several cities around the world and interviewed people regarding love, sex, and marriage. I was so fascinated by the different views of what is acceptable when it comes to love, sex, and marriage. Culture has so much influence on beliefs and behaviors we choose to accept in relationships, including the expectations and sacrifice. Societal norms are ingrained in us, and we know what we are expected to do. I certainly had preconceived notions about love and relationships between couples in other countries.

Perhaps you do as well.

Here are some of the takeaways from the discussions that really stuck out for me:

> The documentary starts out in **Tokyo, Japan**. The reporter is interviewing a group of ladies at a local bar. In this group, some of the women are married and some are single. The married ladies, although hesitant, explained that most Japanese couples have sexless marriages. Once

the children are born, the mothers sleep with the children and the husband sleeps alone. He is free to come and go and has limited responsibility for child rearing. Wives are also very aware that most Japanese men have mistresses or women they have sex with outside of their wives. The married women expressed that they also have "boyfriends." It is widely accepted, and the most important factor is that it is not spoken of. I would call this a "sweep it under the rug" culture.

Universally, Japanese do not feel the need to share everything or expose vulnerability or feelings. This is not to say they don't feel them, but they are extremely private about such affairs. When asked if they would confront the husband about a mistress, the married ladies stated they would never do that, and he would just ignore it altogether anyway if she did. The single ladies, who seemed more modernized in thinking, said they would prefer to find a mate outside of Japan. Unanimously among those interviewed, public displays of affection are seen as disrespectful and lacking moral sense. The Japanese are a very modest and reserved people. Most couples stated they do not say "I love you" or kiss one another.

Next, on to **Delhi, India**. The most common movement in India addressed was the treatment of women. The Posh Act is a recent law to protect women against sexual harassment, which was common in public and never punishable by law previously.

Although arranged marriages are still prevalent, modern-day India is pushing for love marriages. Premarital sex is still considered dishonorable. The people still hold too many old beliefs about how a virgin is considered higher in value, even if money today is not exchanged.

Beirut, Lebanon: Sadly, this interview was painful and heartbreaking to watch as one woman explained how a man is allowed to divorce his wife, at will, at any time. The wife does not have to be notified or present in court. She may suddenly receive a letter in the mail stating her husband has divorced her. The courts will award the husband the divorce, and child custody is never awarded to the mother. In this interview, the Lebanese mother was only allowed to see her two-year-old child one day per week after the divorce. She could not have any part in the schooling or medical care. The child would be allowed to choose which parent they would like to live with when they turned fourteen years old.

Although there were some forward-thinking individuals as well, it seemed rare in this country. Again, these topics are not openly discussed in their culture.

Berlin, Germany: In Germany, the consensus regarding love and sex is divided into the old school ways and the open, liberal attitudes of today. Youths are much more open about talking and exposing information regarding sex.

There were two young ladies interviewed who had a web business of exposing their sexual encounters. They were very confident in their sexuality and believed they had a right to choose to enjoy intimacy with as many partners as desired. They have nude bars and beaches, and the body is not seen as something to cover or feel shame about.

I personally love this culture as it reduces body shaming and allows the freedom to be who you want to be. However, I may be biased toward Germany, as I lived there for several years during my twenties and love the people and country.

Accra, Ghana: I really came away from watching this episode with bafflement but compassion for understanding the "why" of behavior in relationships in this culture. To understand the behavior, we must understand the circumstances.

In Accra, a woman is unable to make enough money to support herself. Getting an apartment requires two years' rent up front. Christianity is the prevalent religion, English is spoken, and it is clearly understood that the man is the head of the family. In this culture, men are revered and have freedom to do as they please.

It is common for a man to have a wife (or two) plus a mistress and a girlfriend. The man will financially support all of the women, and the women are completely aware of one another!

I must admit I felt it was quite a healthy acceptance of their circumstances; at least there wasn't dishonesty and deception. Those married women who were interviewed were very adamant that a woman's sole purpose is to serve the man with food, sex, and a clean house at all times. They did not appear to be resentful; they smiled as they said it and accepted it as the way it is required. One married gentleman was asked if he had relationships with other women and he said, "No, because I am poor. Only the rich men can do that." So, it wasn't a moral issue, it was a financial one.

Finally, the series ended in **Shanghai, China**. I feel as though this was the most surprising of all the places in my misunderstanding of other cultures. As they were walking around the city, the reporter and a local celebrity host of a dating show came across what was called an umbrella market.

There were parents sitting beside upside-down umbrellas scattered all over the ground. In these umbrellas were flyers that described the attributes of their children—level of education, height, weight, background, as well as photographs. These parents were trying to find a mate for their children. When asked if their children knew they were doing it, they declared no.

The culture in China is to have your child marry an ideal partner because they will be taking care of the parents as they age. It is not uncommon to have four generations living under one roof. These parents want to make the best choice for THEMSELVES, not necessarily for their children. You can see that love is an afterthought (or even a non-thought) in relation to the long-term goals of these parents.

A transgender woman indicated how unaccepted LGBTQ individuals are in the country. Married now to a German citizen, she was able to find an understanding and loving man. Her words gave me the perspective that love in China is viewed more as a practicality than an emotion:

"Happiness is a luxury, not 100 percent necessary."

"Love and marriage are separate things: marriage is a job and love is love."

"Traditional Chinese love is about sacrifice" and

"Family is so much more important."

While watching and listening to these planet-sharing souls, at times my chin would drop in shock; other times, I was saddened that happiness seemed the last priority. I realized our circumstances are only dreadful or appalling if we view them that way.

What I find unacceptable may be a way of life and completely normal for others. It always comes down to choices. We can accept and live the cultural principles of our demographics or we can fight for what we truly desire if they are outside of those practices. To acknowledge other peoples' customs, beliefs, and cultures is inclusive and compassionate. Just food for thought as you travel and meet others of different ethnicities.

If you live in a culture where it is allowed, be grateful for having freedom to choose who to love and nurture relationships that are honest and fulfilling.

Chapter 23

ARE YOU INTO IT? OR INTUIT?

Recently, I've noticed something really strange happening with Jade, our chihuahua. She sits on a rug or carpet and looks around as if something is attracting her attention. Picture it as if a fly was buzzing around her, but there is no fly! She is lost in her own thoughts and it really looks as if something is trying to get her attention. If you've ever watched paranormal reality shows or listened to psychic mediums, they explain how messages can be sent by spirits. Animals are known to be highly sensitive to feeling and sensing spirits. I feel as if Jade is sensing something similar. I believe my dogs know how I'm feeling without my use of words. They intuitively sense my energy and mood.

My husband is similar, though—sorry, honey—not quite as adept at it. I joke that we "share a brain." An example of this was while sitting at my desk working one day, I got a craving for Cheetos. That is not a snack I eat often or have handy in our pantry. Dennis was at work, and I didn't tell him or text him about my craving. When he arrived home from work in the evening, he held a bag of Cheetos in his hand! I will admit that was pretty freaky, but we've had similar incidents where I also do the same for him. It's this cool connection that we have on all levels. We just "get" one another.

Here's another of those levels:

One night while relaxing and watching a documentary about the late Jeffrey Epstein, convicted child trafficker and abuser, we both started getting very upset at what we were watching. It evolved into this conversation about life, politics, and wealth.

I realized then that a great area of discussion for this book would be how important it is to be intellectually stimulated by your mate. My parents used to say about my past partners, "You dummied down." In their not-so-gentle-way they were saying: "Find someone you can have interesting discussions with, someone who can contribute intelligently to a conversation."

I've always been a sponge when it came to learning new things, but having a sweetheart who can teach you and even help you see things from different perspective is really fun!

> *"I have never in my life learned anything from any man who agreed with me."*
> *—Dudley Field Malone*

I like that particular quote because it tells us to be open-minded to what others have to say. It's called psychological flexibility or the ability to think, act, and behave in differing ways. We can be curious and non-critical, understanding and non-judgmental. If you approach new people and circumstances with a what-can-I-learn-from-this attitude, life becomes very interesting.

"Intuit," "intuition," and "intuitive" all have varied meanings, but the heart of these words is the *knowing.*

Webster's dictionary definition of intuit:

"to know or understand (something) because of what you feel or sense rather than because of the evidence : to know or understand (something) through intuition."

I believe we all encounter intuitive moments. Those who recognize it most often will be aware and make conscious decisions and choices or, at the least, have some self-awareness questions. There are no coincidences. Everything will be brought to you when you are ready to receive it. I like to call them nudges when we are off track or looking for an answer.

Here are some examples of ways we receive our intuitive messages:

1. You wake up in the morning and you think about an old friend from high school. You have not spoken to this friend in a very long time, and the two of you had a falling out years ago. You temporarily dismiss it and go about your day.

   If you act on the intuition, you could look up the old friend and send a message on social media. It could mean there is some healing needed. Maybe you have held onto guilt over the fallout. Maybe you are trying to be a better friend.

2. As you're driving to the grocery store, a song comes on the radio that you remember your mom singing while she did her chores.

When you hear the song and think of your mother, it may be that she's missing you and wants to spend time together but doesn't want to interfere in your busy life. Or maybe she has passed and she's letting you know to be sure to live life to the fullest and enjoy it before you transition or pass away. Maybe there is a decision to be made and your mom is guiding you to the right one.

3. Suddenly, you remember you were going to have lunch with a new and interesting person you met on Facebook, so you meet at a restaurant and feel as if you have known this person for a very long time.

This new friend may be a soul connection you have met in another life or that God or Source brought into your life for a purpose, to help you heal or connect you to opportunities. Maybe they have experiences that can help you through and vice versa.

We can relate this to the dating process or soulmate search. You know the cliché "listen to your gut." That is intuition. Or "follow your heart"; that is intuitive. I could go on, but you get the idea.

There is a duality in humans that creates this tug-of-war within ourselves. We tend to believe if we are not using logic, we are being silly or living in a fantasy world. Sadly, we miss out on the fun and joy by always needing to be rational, reasoning, and sensible. On the flip side, we still need to use common sense and go with our intuition about feelings that DON'T feel right. If something feels "off," it is.

That's a vibration or attraction that is teaching you something.

So how do you charter these rough waters of knowing the difference?

You just will.

Look back at the past moments in your life where you say to yourself, "I should've known," or "I felt like it was the wrong choice." There are people and things we must experience, and no book or lecture in the world will give us the expertise of living through something.

My own father used to say, "You never listened to me; you could have avoided the situation." To that, I replied just as I'm writing here, "I just had to go through it myself to understand the lesson." We all want to help another avoid pain we have endured, but it's not our job to prevent the lesson another soul is here to learn. It's especially difficult letting it happen for our loved ones.

In a previous chapter about dating, I said not to put the red flags in your bag. In a more spiritual way, I'm stating, "Pay attention to the feelings you are having." Don't disregard it when a phrase or action didn't sit well with you. Or when someone had a very close resemblance to a past difficult relationship.

I met a gentleman (I use this term loosely) online when I was single and dating. We decided to pursue an exclusive relationship for a while. I recall hearing him describe his ex-wife at the beginning of our year together. He talked very negatively and painted a picture of himself as the saint. He had an older daughter as well, and I remember him telling me he had stopped talking to her for a year over a money issue. I also witnessed him ignore his nephew for an extended amount of time for making a joke while golfing together.

Looking back, following my intuition, I should have run fast and far and never looked back. I overlooked many red flags.

As we progressed and moved to cohabitating in my home, he lost his job, moved his daughter in, and neither of them were meeting their financial responsibilities to me for the household expenses. He would get extremely offended if I asked him for payment from his unemployment check and a small amount from his adult daughter, who had a good paying job. He was always a man who lacked generosity with money. He was quite egotistic and selfish.

Bottom line, how did I miss those intuitive messages and clues? Why didn't I walk away at the first signs? I was not aware of what my intuition was saying. I ignored the signs.

Fast-forward to meeting my husband on our first date.

We talked openly and honestly (still do) about everything. The most poignant moment I can recall was his dialogue regarding his ex-wife and the mother of his son. He spoke with so much respect about how well they have co-parented, how they overcame their past hurts and are good friends.

Now THAT got my attention!

Why? Obviously, I had seen the darker side with the other man, so this resonated as a kind, caring, and good man. My intuition told me, "That is a different kind of partner. That man is unselfish and confident." You WILL see and know when you are ready for a relationship. Many times, in hindsight of a failed relationship, we say we are *blindsided*, but that is not true. The truth is, we chose not to see it, and we chose not to look for it. We ignored our intuition.

Many times, when we are single, we want the companionship and relationship so much, we will overlook the flaws or convince ourselves we are too choosy, critical, or finicky. It isn't until you realize you have the choice that you will make the choice. Read that again. Good enough is not enough, and inevitably, you will see it. The determination is when, not if.

Chapter 24

HAVE FAITH,
IT WILL ALL
WORK OUT

People constantly say to avoid two subjects in conversation if you want to avoid conflict: religion and politics. Politics is not something that relates to my puppies and is definitely out. I also debated internally if I should approach the subject of religion in this book. I feel I would be doing a disservice to myself and my readers if I didn't share my honesty about all subjects—at the very least, offer a perspective to consider.

As I was thinking of a way to relate religion to my dogs, I concluded that it would seem a stretch of logic, since they really don't seem to care much about such things. However, as I thought about religion, it became clear that the underlying reason behind faith, once again, comes down to belief.

Brodie has a very thick coat of fur. Since we live in Arizona, the weather gets extremely hot in the summer. I always wish he would go in the pool, but he is extremely afraid of it. By my son's own admission, he had tossed Brodie in the pool several times when he was a puppy, hoping to get him to swim and enjoy it, and he has been afraid since. Even if I coax him to come close to the pool's edge, he is scared and won't let me touch him.

Even though he trusts me, and I have earned this trust over years, he still has an inherent belief that it is not something he desires to do, no matter how hot he is. He has been this way since he was a puppy, and he's nine years old. Much like us, possibly he remembers an experience in his youth or even going to the groomer for a bath routinely, and he hasn't been able to overcome his water fears.

Most of our beliefs stem from the programming and observation of our parents, friends, and media. Whether we will repeat what we learned or choose to do differently is strictly up to us.

In my family, my mother was raised Catholic and even attended Catholic school. On the complete opposite end of the spectrum, my father decided at a young age that he did not believe in God, church, or religion. He used to have to walk in the snow by himself to Sunday school each week and decided one day he did not like church. Whether from experience or choice, this is where they stood in their faith beliefs. I wonder if early on as a couple they had discussed how they would compromise, once married, and choose how to raise their children on this subject.

The simple answer is that they chose to let us make up our own minds. We did not attend church, but we were never stifled in being allowed to explore options. I think it was a healthy choice. I explored a lot of different churches with friends and attended my grandparents' Lutheran church. I've since evolved from religion to spirituality, believing it's a much bigger picture than I had known. My own experiences expanded what my beliefs are today. As humans, we spend a lot of time trying to convince one another through logic, scientific theory, or our own revelations to join in our beliefs. I do think everyone needs something to believe that brings them joy and hope. The bottom line? Do what makes you happy.

In relation to finding a good fit for us, it is important to ask these questions and address the subjects of faith and religion with someone you meet, date, or marry. This is one of those subjects that can be a dealbreaker to some as it is a passionate and deep-seated part of who we are. It can be a part of the compromises within your relationship, just like my parents did. Others will choose to convert to their partners' faith, while still others find a way to adapt the beliefs of both partners in their children's lives. In contrast, it might not be an important attribute to someone when seeking love partners. The most important point is that it should be addressed up front and agreed upon without judgment of one another.

I had asked a reader once to write a review for my first book, and they responded that they follow the Bible and cannot do that. I was taken aback at this explanation. I did not feel my writing was in any way disparaging their Christianity belief, as I discuss God, Spirit, and a higher power. Therefore, it was more about the writing review and what positive things they had obtained from reading the book. It honestly baffled me, but I respected their opinion.

Whatever your religious beliefs, whether Christianity, metaphysical, agnostic or atheism, Buddhism, Hinduism, and the list goes on—if that's what gives you hope and brings you peace and joy, then it is completely your decision and choice.

We are all entitled to our opinion and belief and should not judge one another for opposing views.

I wrote this blog on my website and it sums up how I desire that we should all live, as open-minded individuals, and realize that we are all wanting and needing the same things out of this life.

"*We are all saying the same thing*"—Blog post Life Coach Maureen website, February 27, 2020

Something has really come to my attention lately. It's been inserting itself over and over in my daily life.

I'm certain you are similar to myself in that when you wake up in the morning, you scroll through your social media accounts and see memes, motivational quotes, and videos. Your friends post about their lives and businesses and ask for prayers for themselves or family members.

If you watch TEDx videos, listen to podcasts, or even watch the Google commercial from the NFL Superbowl, you can't help but notice that the message is the same. Enjoy your life and be happy! This is the very simplified version...so let's go further.

I recently attended two different seminars that caught my attention. They were about how to be successful in your business.

As I sat in these seminars, I made this huge revelation that we are all saying the same things because we all WANT the same things! I've made my own speeches, written the same variations of ideas in blogs, and included the concept in my first book, *My Dog Is More Enlightened Than I Am.*

Here are some quote examples from celebrities and prominent leaders that cement this idea:

Dalai Lama: *"When we are born, we have no idea of nationality or religious faith. We are just human beings who want to be happy."*

Mother Teresa: *"The most terrible poverty is loneliness, and the feeling of being unloved."*

Jim Carrey: *"When you compromise and fail, it hurts worse than failing at what you love."*

Mahatma Gandhi: *"Be the change you want to see in the world."*

Christopher Reeve: *"Once you choose hope, anything's possible."*

Albert Einstein: *"A true sign of intelligence is not knowledge but imagination."*

Lucille Ball: *"Love yourself first and everything else falls into line. You really have to love yourself to get anything done in this world."*

All of these inspirational, talented, and spiritual beings are essentially saying the same things, regardless of differing religions, backgrounds, occupations, or beliefs.

If I may be so bold as to sum up the thousands of years of human existence to these below ideas that recirculate throughout time in different languages, cultures, and religions, it is this:

We are here to accept, validate, help, support, forgive, be compassionate and love **one another**. We are co-creating in each generation to make the next one better.

To introduce new ideas and larger views of the world around us. If we remove the barriers of religion, politics, and childhood programming, we are a conglomerate of amazing innovators. Be open to ideas and views of others.

> *"I have never in my life learned anything from any man who agreed with me."* Dudley Field Malone

We have a purpose here. It is to **learn, grow, accept, create, enhance, forgive, believe, expand, and love ourselves**! We grow from the experiences we have asked for. The greater the pain, the greater the lesson. You do not want to leave this earth as the same person you came as. You want your years to have counted. Your "dash" (time between birth and death on your headstone) should be a legacy that lives on in those you have interacted with and loved.

When you go out into your day today, whatever you hear and see, look through the viewfinder of "We are all saying the same thing."

In closing this book, I will leave you with the knowledge and belief that you can find, keep, nurture, and deserve a perfect love relationship. Humans are here for relationships; without them, we are not fulfilling our purpose of bettering mankind or expanding our souls. Whether it is your choice or not, you must interact with others. Learning the effectiveness of communication, trust, and compassion will be the difference between the best connections you have with your fellow humans and your most treasured soul family and friends.

Maureen Scanlon, November 1, 2020

MUST-HAVE CHARACTERISTICS

_____

_____

_____

_____

_____

_____

_____

_____

_____

_____

_____

_____

_____

_____

_____

_____

_____

_____

_____

_____

_____

_____

_____

_____

_____

_____

_____

CHARACTERISTICS I DESIRE

-FIN-

Chapter 9 - Entertain Yourself

Every morning the puppies, Brodie and Jade, and I have a routine. We go downstairs, I make coffee, feed them their three-course breakfast, and we head out to the backyard. Some mornings when we go outside, there are stuffed animal babies lying all over the yard. It makes me giggle, because sometime between evening and morning, one or both of them came out and started playing. Just random, fun play. It makes me wonder why humans get bored. Have you ever seen a bored dog? No, because they are either playing or sleeping. That's what we should view our day as...two categories. Sleep or Play. Who's with me?

1. **How do you play?** I am constantly asking people, what do you enjoy? What's your passion? I'm not talking about work passion, family passion, etc. But really more about what do you enjoy doing? Do you draw, knit, hike, or cook?

   We seem to always be on electronic gadgets for entertainment. I know it's a generational gap, but as a kid in the eighties, we found stuff to do. We created worlds out of everyday places and items. It's very therapeutic to lose yourself in a project. Whether you are "crafty" or not, there are some easy kits at every hobby store. Go for a walk and take pictures of nature on your phone. Buy a used piece of furniture and repaint it. If there's something you've never done before and have always wanted to do, sign up for a class and learn how to do it! Everyone needs downtime and moments to be alone to enjoy their serenity and seclusion from all that goes on daily in our lives.

Take time for yourself and play!

CPSIA information can be obtained
at www.ICGtesting.com
Printed in the USA
FSHW021353150222
88233FS